MADE IN MADAGASCAR

MADE IN MADAGASCAR

SAPPHIRES, ECOTOURISM, AND THE GLOBAL BAZAAR

ANDREW WALSH

Teaching Culture: UTP Ethnographies for the Classroom

UNIVERSITY OF TORONTO PRESS

Copyright © University of Toronto Press Incorporated 2012
Higher Education Division

www.utppublishing.com

Library and Archives Canada Cataloguing in Publication

Walsh, Andrew, 1969–

        Made in Madagascar : sapphires, ecotourism, and the global bazaar / Andrew Walsh.

(Teaching culture)
Includes bibliographical references and index.
Issued also in electronic formats.
ISBN 978-1-4426-0374-5

        1. Sapphires—Economic aspects—Madagascar—Ankarana Special Reserve.
2. Ecotourism—Economic aspects—Madagascar—Ankarana Special Reserve. 3. Bazaars
(Markets)—Madagascar. 4. Globalization—Madagascar. 5. Madagascar—Economic conditions.
6. Madagascar—Social conditions. 7. Ethnology—Madagascar. 8. Anthropology—Madagascar.
I. Title. II. Series: Teaching culture

HC895.W24 2012   330.9691'05   C2012-905272-8

We welcome comments and suggestions regarding any aspect of our publications—please
feel free to contact us at news@utphighereducation.com or visit our Internet site at
www.utppublishing.com.

North America   UK, Ireland, and continental Europe
5201 Dufferin Street   NBN International
North York, Ontario, Canada, M3H 5T8   Estover Road, Plymouth, PL6 7PY, UK
                                       ORDERS PHONE: 44 (0) 1752 202301
2250 Military Road   ORDERS FAX: 44 (0) 1752 202333
Tonawanda, New York, USA, 14150   ORDERS E-MAIL: enquiries@nbninternational.com

ORDERS PHONE: 1-800-565-9523
ORDERS FAX: 1-800-221-9985
ORDERS E-MAIL: utpbooks@utpress.utoronto.ca

The University of Toronto Press acknowledges the financial support for its publishing activities of
the Government of Canada through the Canada Book Fund.

Cover design and interior by Em Dash Design.

For Karin, with thanks.

CONTENTS

PREFACE

This book was written with undergraduate students in mind. Although it includes the specificities one would expect to find in any ethnographic case study, I have organized it in a way that instructors will find conducive to teaching a wide range of topics and approaches.

The Introduction invites readers to google "Madagascar" and other key terms on which the book focuses. In highlighting what comes of online searches like these, I offer a brief overview of the chapters to come in a way that is intended to have readers think carefully about the limits of what the Internet can tell us about our interconnected world. As I stress early on, Google is useful only when you know what you're looking for.

Chapter 1, "The Place of the Rocks," introduces Ankarana, the region of northern Madagascar where the research discussed took place. To illustrate the various, complex, and influential perspectives to be considered in the chapters that follow, I focus in particular on three ways in which people approach this region and "the rocks" (a huge limestone massif) at its centre: as a sacred place of tombs and shared history, as a natural wonder worthy of protection through conservation efforts, and as a place of opportunity for settlers and prospectors of various stripes. The chapter concludes with a discussion of why anthropologists often argue that seemingly out-of-the-way places like Ankarana ought to be central in our efforts to understand the workings of our interconnected world. Instructors may find the content of this chapter relevant to broader discussions of anthropological research methods, traditional political organization, taboos, environmental anthropology, political ecology, and globalization.

Chapter 2, "Living in the Wake of Sapphires," discusses Ankarana's sapphire trade, focusing specifically on the social, political, and economic processes that give life in a northern Malagasy mining town its particular contours: the risking and daring involved in mining work, the buying and selling involved in trading, and the gifting and grifting that shape and threaten social relationships. The chapter concludes with a discussion of the speculating that people in Ankarana's sapphire trade do about the global markets served by their work, suggesting that such speculating *about* sapphires must be understood in light of the speculating *in* sapphires that occupies so many of them. Instructors may find the content of this chapter relevant to broader discussions of work, exchange, social organization, the cultural construction of gender, commodity circulation, consumption, materiality, and world view.

Chapter 3, "The Promise and Practice of Ecotourism," discusses the great but seemingly unrealizable potential of tourism in Ankarana, focusing in particular on the development of the region's ecotourist trade and on the specifics of the work of Malagasy guides, who have been among this trade's few local beneficiaries. The chapter closes by considering the speculations that many in the region have about foreign visitors and stresses, once again, the value of taking such speculations seriously by understanding them as suggestive of some of the more obvious aspects of ecotourism that are often overlooked. Instructors may find the content of this chapter relevant to broader discussions of conservation, sustainable development, neoliberalism, cross-cultural communication, and the political and economic inequalities that characterize our interconnected world.

Chapter 4, "Natural Wonders in the Global Bazaar," discusses the commodification of what I term Ankarana's "natural wonders," focusing on insights that come from considering the similar ways in which foreign consumers value the region's sapphires and its ecotourist attractions. I argue that the two might be understood as distinctive in two ways: both as unique and essentially authentic one-of-a-kind vessels of naturalness, and as generic and largely interchangeable commodities that gain their economic value through inclusion in what I term the "global bazaar." The global bazaar, I suggest, offers a world of options to consumers and a world of marginalizing paradoxes to people in places like Ankarana. Instructors may find the content of this chapter relevant to broader discussions of multi-sited research, the "resource curse," commodity chains, value, authenticity, tourism, religion, and the cultural construction of "nature."

The Conclusion offers a final take on how connections being made in the global bazaar today systematically value and devalue the work of people at the sources of the world's most valued commodities. I illustrate this point by discussing how several recent crises have affected people working in

Ankarana's sapphire and ecotourist trades and then conclude, reflexively, with a consideration of how this book is itself a product of the forces it professes to be about. Instructors may find this final discussion especially useful for engaging students in reflection and discussion on the dilemmas that come with doing anthropology today.

Some of the key arguments of this book were developed previously in my other publications listed in the References. Certain passages from Chapters 2, 3, and 4 and the Conclusion appeared previously in Walsh (2003, 2004, 2005, and 2010).

ACKNOWLEDGMENTS

The research on which this book is based would not have been possible without funding from the Social Sciences and Humanities Research Council of Canada and the Wenner-Gren Foundation for Anthropological Research. Additional support from the London School of Economics, Mount Allison University, Wilfrid Laurier University, the University of Western Ontario, and the Laboratoire d'Anthropologie Sociale is also gratefully acknowledged.

I am indebted to a great many colleagues whose comments, collaboration, and mentorship have been essential to the various research projects in which this book originated, in particular Rita Astuti, Martelline Be Razafindravola, Laurent Berger, Maurice Bloch, Scott Cardiff, Alexis Chapeskie, Tom Cushman, Louis-Philippe D'Arvisenet, Gillian Feeley-Harnik, Elizabeth Ferry, Lisa Gezon, Les Field, Ben Freed, Paul Hanson, Richard Hughes, Emma Hunter, Eva Keller, David Meyers, Ashley Patterson, Tahosy Radaniarison, Marie-Alette Soameva, Emmanuel Tehindrazanarivelo, Peter Traviza, Christi Turner, and Paige West. I am especially grateful to Michael Lambek for years of support, good advice, and friendship. I have also benefited greatly from the support and encouragement of colleagues at Mount Allison University, Wilfrid Laurier University, and the University of Western Ontario. Special thanks to Ian Colquhoun, Alex Totomarovario, and the many Canadian and Malagasy students and colleagues who have participated in the University of Western Ontario/Université d'Antsiranana research and student exchange program. All royalties generated by this book will fund the ongoing participation of Malagasy students in this program.

Thanks to John Barker, Paul Hanson, Jim Igoe, Dan Jorgensen, and Eva Keller, who read and commented on a draft of the manuscript. Any shortcomings are my own responsibility. Thanks also to the staff of University of Toronto Press, and to Anne Brackenbury in particular, for their support, guidance, and patience.

I have three families to thank. The first is the one in Madagascar that has taken me in: a family of different names and roles (Morafeno, D'Arvisenet, *zama, vavo, zoky, zandry, asidy, valy, dadilahy, dady, mama*, and *baba*) that grows with every visit. The second is the family I have made with Karin, Catherine, and Theresa: a family that now extends to a growing number of Schwerdtners. Most important, though, thanks are due to my mother, Ann (Coughlin) Walsh, and my father, John Walsh, who have provided a family of precious relations and inspirational ways of relating.

I am indebted to far more individuals in Ankarana than I can hope to list here. While based in Ambatoharanana, I was taken in by hosts, parents, and siblings from all factions of a complex family. I am especially grateful to Karima, to Tsimiharo III, and to all of the Ankarabe. While based in Ambondromifehy, I benefited especially from the hospitality and generosity of Zaman'Tombozandry and Maman'Doxy, and of Ampanjaka and Kosy. In Mahamasina, I found a third Ankarana home with Baban'Tarsis and Maman'Tarsis, and with Baban'Nana and Maman'Nana—great hosts and friends. More broadly, I am clearly indebted to the hundreds of people in Ankarana who have invited me to sit, to eat, and to talk over the years. As noted in the Conclusion, it is their generous participation that has made this book what it is.

All names in the text that follows are pseudonyms.

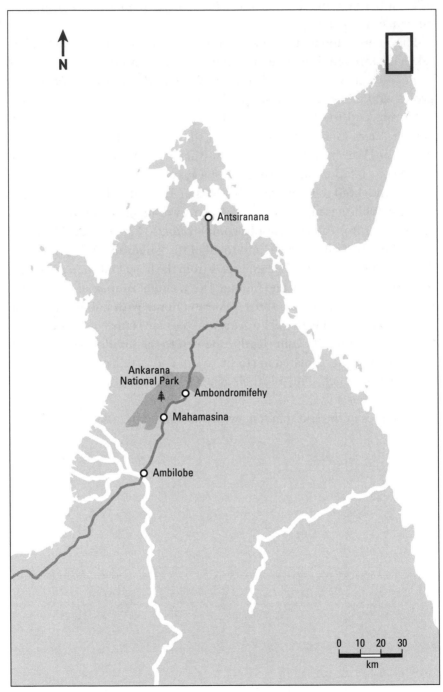

Northern Madagascar

INTRODUCTION: LINKS

Google "Madagascar." Go ahead ... try it. Today I got back over 50,000,000 links. For some readers, the most familiar of the top ten will lead to sites associated with the movie that has taken the country's name as its title. Fight the urge to follow the familiar. Do that other thing that Google enables: consider what you don't know.

The first link that comes up when I google "Madagascar" from Canada leads to a Wikipedia entry devoted to the country. Here you'll find what this and other encyclopedic sites like it tend to offer: a collection of facts, figures, images, generalizations, and bits of trivia. Wikipedia informs us, for example, that Madagascar is the fourth-largest island in the world, that it is home to 5 per cent of the world's plant and animal species, and that it was a colony of France from 1896 to 1960 (Wikipedia n.d.). Farther down in my search results, a CIA World Factbook report on the country notes that Madagascar has 4,828 kilometres of coastline, that only 5 per cent of its more than 480,000 square kilometres of land is arable, and that 30 per cent of its more than 20 million inhabitants live in towns and cities (CIA World Factbook 2012). Madagascar is not, in other words, the uninhabited "wild" that many—animated characters included—imagine it to be. Nor is it a paradise of plenty. Still farther down my list of links, UNICEF's most recent country report indicates that more than one in twenty Malagasy children die before the age of five, that the average life expectancy for a Malagasy person is 66 years, and that the per-capita gross national income is US$440 per year (UNICEF 2012). I could go on.

As someone who went through high school and most of university without the Internet, I'm old enough to marvel at how a search engine can generate so much information from so little effort. I'd like to think that if

I *had* had access to the Internet back in 1992, when I was first offered the opportunity to conduct anthropological research in Madagascar, I might have known more about the country at the time than where to find it on a map. The truth is, however, that even with the Internet, I would probably have known as little about the place as do most of the people I meet in Canada today. Google is wonderful when you know what you are looking for, but it isn't much of a teacher.

This book offers links that Google could never generate on its own. Specifically, it describes the links that might be drawn between northern Madagascar's sapphire and ecotourist trades, as well as the links that connect participants in these trades to the foreign consumers served by their work. More generally, and ambitiously, it aspires to get across links of a sort that anthropologists often try to teach: links that connect familiar and unfamiliar realities, reveal unexpected associations and unconsidered entanglements, and encourage new ways of thinking about what ties and divides people in a shared world. To establish the links I have in mind, it makes sense to start by chipping away at the unfamiliar with some fundamentals.

Search: Madagascar

Madagascar is an island. Around 200 million years ago, its landmass was located in the middle of Gondwanaland, the prehistoric supercontinent from which South America, Africa, Australia, and other continents of the southern hemisphere originate. Over tens of millions of years, it split off from its place between what are now the east coast of Africa and the south-west coast of India, winding up disconnected from the rest of the world in the midst of the Indian Ocean. Set apart in this way, Madagascar hosted the evolution of a great number of distinctive plant and animal species. Take one look at the aye-aye (a species of primate), the uroplatus (a kind of gecko), or any of the six species of baobab trees found only in Madagascar and you'll get some sense of what millions of years of isolation can do for the development of flora and fauna in a place.

People arrived in Madagascar only recently, some time within the past 2,000 years, and with them came dramatic changes to the island's ecosystems. People require land on which to farm, meat to eat, fuel for cooking, and wood for building, and the existing ecosystems have always supplied such fundamental human needs for those living there. Over the past 500 years, the island has also supplied a long list of internationally traded commodities—vanilla, cloves, cotton, sugar, tortoise shell, gold, tropical hardwood, and, in recent years, oil, gemstones, and industrial minerals—the production or extraction of which has required Malagasy people to work the land around them in ways driven by the demand of distant consumers. With these points in mind, it makes little sense to blame the island's current, and much discussed, "environmental crisis" (Kaufmann 2006) on its residents. That Madagascar's distinctive biodiversity appears to be under threat in the early twenty-first century is attributable ultimately to the island's relatively recent and rapid jump from being one of the most isolated to one of the most connected places in the world, from the slow track of gradual geological and evolutionary processes to the fast track of global migration and trade routes.

Madagascar's first human inhabitants came from Southeast Asia. The most compelling evidence of such origins is found in the Malagasy language, classified by linguists as being of Austronesian origin and thus in a category that also includes indigenous languages of Taiwan, Hawaii, and the Philippines. Malagasy people are nevertheless not as homogenous as their common language suggests. Some sources even propose that the people of Madagascar might be neatly divided up into 18 tribes or ethnic groups, each with its own distinctive history, customs, and homeland. If only Malagasy people, past or present, were so easily categorized in reality (see Eggert 1986, Esoavelomandroso 1989, and Astuti 1995, for example). In fact, the Malagasy people I know are no different from any people I know in Canada in associating and affiliating with one another in many different ways: as members of families, participants in community organizations, devotees of religious congregations, and, of course, practitioners of different kinds of work, to name just a few.

The deeper you get into a search for information about Madagascar, the clearer it becomes that everything Google might tell you about this place has been shaped by the perspectives of those representing it. Nowhere is this simple fact more evident than in the long list of labels and alternative names by which Madagascar has come to be known by foreigners over the years. Some designations, like "the great red island" (Stratton 1965) and "the island of megadiversity" (Wildlife Conservation Society n.d.), refer to the distinctive geography, flora, and fauna of the place, while others, like "island of the ancestors" (Mack 1986), call attention to the distinctive culture and beliefs of the people living there. Some monikers reference Madagascar's natural and cultural otherworldliness, referring to it variously as "a world apart" (PBS n.d.), "a world out of time" (Lanting 1990), and a "lost world" (Tyson 2000), while others, like "vanilla island" (Nomadic Thoughts n.d.), call to mind its longstanding history as a well-connected centre of global trade. Even *National Geographic* can't seem to decide on a single label, classifying it among the world's "last great places" in one of its many publications (*National Geographic* n.d.), and calling it an "environmental hell" in another (Bellows 2001). Clearly, whatever sources like these tell us about Madagascar, they tell us even more about how outsiders imagine the place.

How, then, does Madagascar appear within Madagascar? Googling "Madagascar" from the country's own home page (www.google.mg) provides a list of links that look quite different to those I get when googling from Canada. The top results here will take you to governmental websites, social networking sites, classified ads, and online editions of newspapers, and thus much closer to the Madagascar that I have come to know from spending time there since 1992. Madagascar is a country of workers and citizens, of social people looking to connect and exchange with one another, and of consequential current events. In other words, Madagascar is in many ways not so different from the places you know best. I should be careful not to overstate my own knowledge of the island, however. Most of the three years I have spent living and doing research there has taken place in just one region: Ankarana, or "the place of the rocks."

Search: Madagascar and Ankarana

Searching "Madagascar and Ankarana" from the Google images portal will provide links to dozens of pictures of "the rocks" from which the Ankarana region of northern Madagasar takes its name. The rocks in question are those of the Ankarana massif, a 25-kilometre-long limestone plateau featuring cliffs, caves, and other sites spectacular enough to have been featured in nature documentaries, distinctive enough to be at the centre of a National Park, and accessible enough to be found all over the Internet in the Flickr sets and YouTube clips of foreign visitors.

It is an amazing place. In satellite images, the Ankarana massif looks like little more than a smudge on the northernmost tip of Madagascar, but on the ground it appears to erupt out of the surrounding savannah, its distinctive limestone pinnacles—called *tsingy* in Malagasy—shooting skyward and sharing space with specially adapted vegetation. Among biologists and botanists, the massif is perhaps best known for its extensive network of caves, underground rivers, and forests, all of which contain a range of distinctive and co-adapted species of plants and animals; the website of Madagascar's National Parks service promises visitors to Ankarana National Park 330 known species of plant life, 96 species of birds, 60 species of reptiles and amphibians, 14 species of bats, and 11 species of lemurs (Madagascar National Parks n.d.). Ankarana is more than just an oasis of biodiversity, however. For many Malagasy people living in the region, the Ankarana massif is first and foremost a cultural and historical landmark. Indeed, throughout Madagascar, Ankarana is probably best known not for its natural wonders but for the people who take their name from this place: the Antankarana, or "the people of the place of the rocks."

I first travelled to Ankarana in 1992, not to see "the rocks" but to spend time with the people "of" them. Indeed, as I discuss further in Chapter 1, my first trip into the caves mentioned above was not spent marvelling at *tsingy*, stalactites, and underground rivers, but doing my best to avoid these obstacles in order to keep up with thousands of Antankarana pilgrims on their way to visit sacred sites found within the Ankarana massif. In the years since that first visit, I have expanded my research focus in the region to include people who have come to rely on Ankarana not as a sacred cultural landmark but as a place of opportunity—a place in which to mine sapphires, for example, or to find work as a guide for foreign ecotourists. Most of what I present in this book comes from this latter line of research—research based in and around two highway-side communities located just east of the Ankarana massif: the first a sapphire-mining town called Ambondromifehy and the second a regional ecotourism hub called Mahamasina (see map, p. xiv).

When I first came to know Ambondromifehy in 1999, it had just recently exploded from a small roadside village of around 400 inhabitants into a sapphire-mining and -trading boomtown of around 15,000. By that time, thousands of Malagasy migrant miners had been digging illegally within the boundaries of the nearby Ankarana National Park for two years already, and hundreds of Malagasy traders were buying and selling sapphires along the town's main drag; all locally mined and traded sapphires were destined ultimately, as they still are, for foreign exporters and markets. In Chapter 2, I discuss some of the distinctive complexities of work and social life in the midst of such a boom. I should state up front, however, that some of the most interesting things I learned during my time in Ambondromifehy came not from the answers that people gave to questions I was asking, but, rather, from the questions that these same people were asking of me. Most thought-provoking were questions regarding the ultimate destinations and uses of locally mined sapphires: Where do they go after they leave Ankarana? What do foreigners do with them? Perhaps, some speculated, these little blue stones were essential to the production of the electronics that foreign traders brought with them. Or maybe they were used to make nuclear weapons. All that people in Ambondromifehy could be sure of was that sapphires were worth a great deal more to foreigners than they were to Malagasy people.

Ambondromifehy's miners and traders didn't need to go far to observe the exotic consumption habits of foreigners. In fact, they didn't need to leave town. From the earliest years of Ankarana's sapphire boom, truckloads of foreign ecotourists regularly sped through Ambondromifehy on their way to the nearby entrance of Ankarana National Park, located only 20 kilometres to the south in a community called Mahamasina. As you might imagine, Malagasy miners' and traders' observations of, and encounters with, these tourists provided plenty of fuel for speculation. Who were these foreigners, they wondered, and why were they so interested in visiting Ankarana? More specifically, why were these foreigners being welcomed into the sapphire-rich caves and forests of Ankarana National Park while local miners were being chased out? Was this just a coincidence, or could it be that the foreigners travelling *into* the park were after the same thing as the foreigners for whom sapphires coming *out* of the park were ultimately destined?

It would be a mistake to take the questions and conspiracy theories I was hearing in Ambondromifehy as indications of how people living there were confused, disconnected or otherwise out of it. Indeed, viewed from the roadside anywhere in Ankarana, certain workings of the global economy couldn't have been more obvious. The fact that wealthy and relatively more powerful foreigners value, and want access to, what can be found inside Ankarana National Park has been apparent to the region's inhabitants for more than 50 years; in recent decades, this fact has become even clearer in light of the high prices that foreign buyers will pay for seemingly useless stones coming out of this place, and from the expensive trips that foreigners make into it. The questions they ask and speculations they propose in the face of this unfolding reality, then, are not merely indications of what they *don't* know about the wider world. Rather, in the chapters that follow, I consider such questions and speculations as indications of these people's efforts at understanding a paradox that couldn't be clearer: how is it, they wonder, that Malagasy people working in this region can benefit so little from living in the midst of what wealthy foreigners value so highly?

In Chapter 4, I suggest that one way of making sense of this paradox is by understanding it as a systemic feature of the global economy that Ankarana's inhabitants share with the foreign consumers who take such an interest in what this region has to offer. For such an argument to make sense, though, it is important to consider just what it is that foreigners are finding in Ankarana that is so special.

Search: Madagascar and Sapphires

If you search "Madagascar and sapphires" on YouTube, the links that appear give a pretty good sense of the extremes of the global sapphire trade. One sort of video you'll find here depicts the working and living conditions of sapphire miners in different regions of the island. Here you'll see the cramped tunnels in which Ambondromifehy's miners work by candlelight, the rhythmic shovelling of young men digging out a huge sapphire pit in southern Madagascar, and some of the ingenious techniques that Malagasy miners have improvised in the absence of the expensive water and air pumps that would make their work safer and more efficient. Another sort of video you'll find here shows the final product of all this work: cut and polished natural sapphires, either offered up to admirers for magnified examination, or, more often, mounted in jewellery for sale by online and cable TV retailers such as the Home Shopping Network. If you take note of the high prices of what is being sold in the latter videos, you will have some sense of why so much effort is being expended in the former. Simply put, there is a great deal of money to be made in the multi-billion-dollar international gemstone trade.

Madagascar has long been known as a source of precious and semi-precious gemstones. As several gemologists have reminded me over the years, before the prehistoric tectonic shifts that put the island in the place it occupies today, its landmass fit alongside those of southeastern Africa and India, regions long famed for their coloured gemstones. That noted, Madagascar's current sapphire boom is a relatively recent development. International traders took notice of Ankarana only in the 1990s, setting off a rush that I will discuss extensively in the first two chapters. Not long after, much larger, international headline-grabbing sapphire rushes enveloped several regions in the south of the island, and, by the turn of the millennium, Madagascar had earned the reputation as one of the world's most important sources of sapphires. If you or someone you know has bought a piece of sapphire jewellery in recent years, there is a good chance that the sapphire in it came from Madagascar.

As you might guess from the contents of the videos described above, the day-to-day concerns of people involved in Ankarana's sapphire trade are quite far removed from those of foreign consumers of sapphire jewellery.

Many of the questions that people living in Ambondromifehy have faced are those you'd expect to find in any small-scale (sometimes called "artisanal") mining town like this: "Where to dig?," for example, or "To whom do you sell?" The town's inhabitants have also faced questions that come with living among fellow prospectors and relative strangers—"Who can you trust?," for example, and "For how long?" As the boom subsided through the 2000s, and the local trade went into decline, inhabitants found themselves wondering if, and when, they should give up on sapphires and move on to something else. As of 2012, Ambondromifehy isn't dead yet, however. Sapphire mining and trading in the region in the 2010s may not offer people the life-changing opportunities that it did in the late 1990s, but for many of the several thousand left in the town, working in Ankarana's sapphire trade remains among the most attractive of a short list of options. So long as there are people in the world who want to buy the region's sapphires, I was told on my last visit, there will be people in Ambondromifehy to mine and trade them.

Since the earliest years of Ankarana's sapphire rush, Ankarana National Park has provided Ambondromifehy's miners with their most productive worksites. Although off-limits to large-scale mining operations, the park has always been easily accessible to miners willing to defy police and conservation workers' efforts at keeping them out. Not surprisingly, then, Ankarana's sapphire miners have been branded by some as enemies of conservation. In one *National Geographic* article, for example, miners working inside the Ankarana National Park are portrayed as "fortune hunters" who have been "hunting lemurs and other endangered species to feed themselves" and have "stripped and scoured the land, increasing soil erosion and damaging the watershed" (*National Geographic* 2002). Sapphire mining is inherently destructive and unsustainable, the argument goes, and it poses a threat to the conservation of Ankarana's unique ecosystems. That the commodity being pursued inside Ankarana National Park appears to be as frivolous as the biodiversity found in this same place is irreplaceable only makes the threat posed by mining appear more senseless to some, especially those who imagine that there are far better ways in which people in Ankarana might capitalize on the region's "natural" bounty.

Search: Madagascar and Ecotourism

If you google "Madagascar and ecotourism," the highest ranking of the links returned will connect you to sites promoting the island's booming ecotourist industry. Here you'll find the site of an eco-tour operator offering two-week junkets through Madagascar's national parks, a posting from a travel blogger as impressed by the country's beaches as by its leaping lemurs, and a newspaper article trumpeting ecotourism as a potential saviour of Madagascar's endangered biodiversity. Don't let pictures of out-of-the-way places and promises of getting away from it all fool you, however. Over the past several decades, ecotourism has become big business in Madagascar—one of the island's biggest, in fact. Between 1990 and 2001, the number of foreign visitors to Madagascar increased more than fourfold, from 40,000 to over 170,000 (Peypoch et al. 2012: 1231). Following a dip that accompanied an island-wide political crisis in 2002, this trend continued into the new millennium, with numbers of foreign visitors to the country increasing steadily from 139,000 in 2003 to over 277,000 in 2005 (Freudenberger 2010). Following another dip brought on by a 2009 national political crisis, the numbers are on the rise again—in 2012, the Malagasy Ministry of Tourism expects that the country will welcome nearly 250,000 foreign visitors (*L'Express de Madagascar* 2012).

Numbers don't do justice to the changes that a booming tourist industry has brought to Madagascar. Having seen this boom first hand, I can offer some more telling anecdotal indicators. On my first trip through northern Madagascar's provincial capital city of Antsiranana, for example, the nicest hotel in town was La Rascasse, a run-down leftover from the 1960s with a sidewalk bar that seemed always to be taken up by sunburned merchant marines. Today, the city boasts at least a dozen high-end hotels, the most luxurious of all being Le Grand Hotel, a complex that features a casino, a pool with swim-up bar, and a continental breakfast that costs only a little less than what one would have paid for a night at La Rascasse. And that's just a start. The past 15 years have also seen the development of the island's first all-inclusive beach resorts, the renovation of its international airports, and, most significantly here, the development of ecotourism infrastructure in and around the country's growing number of conservation areas. In Ankarana, it was the community of Mahamasina that changed most as a result of Madagascar's ecotourism boom. While Ambondromifehy was booming as a result of the region's sapphire trade, Mahamasina was becoming established as the *de facto* main entrance to Ankarana National Park—a convenient roadside location at which foreign visitors could buy the permits, hire the guides, and stock up on the supplies they would need to discover the marvels of the Ankarana massif.

Madagascar's popularity as an ecotourist destination has developed alongside increasing international awareness of, and concern about, the island's status as what Conservation International calls a "biodiversity hotspot" (Conservation International n.d.). As I discuss in Chapter 3, the country's ecotourism industry has also been the product of a great deal of planning and effort by representatives of the Malagasy state, national, and international conservation organizations, and international lenders and donors. Promoters argue that ecotourism offers a means for protecting the island's unique ecosystems by providing people living in communities around National Parks and other protected areas with opportunities for work and incentives for becoming more conservation minded. If wealthy foreigners are willing to pay for the privilege of visiting undisturbed Malagasy environments, the argument goes, Malagasy people might reasonably hope to be compensated for helping them to do so and will thus have good reason for keeping such places undisturbed.

A number of Malagasy people in Ankarana have done very well from the growth of ecotourism in the region. For some, work in the ecotourism industry has even brought with it just what advocates hoped it would: not only work opportunities, but also an appreciation of the need to conserve the endangered plants, animals, and landscapes that foreigners come to Madagascar to see. That noted, these direct beneficiaries of ecotourism are in the minority in Ankarana. They are nowhere near as numerous, for example, as the thousands of men and women who have sought and found opportunities in the region's sapphire trade over the past 15 years. There is simply no comparison; and yet comparing is just what many seem inclined to do. For those drawn to the region's spectacular biodiversity, certainly, attributing praise and blame in a place like this seems easy to do. On the one hand you have Malagasy people who make their living from ecotourism—exemplars of responsible environmental stewardship who have chosen to embrace the goals and ethos of conservation with an admirable entrepreneurial spirit. On the other you have sapphire miners and traders, people accused of ripping the region's precious landscape apart in search of treasure and profit. The truth is, however, that on the ground shared by Ankarana's ecoguides, miners, park guards, and gem traders, the work that makes a person either a conservationist hero or a short-sighted criminal in the eyes of others is similar in more than one way. Most relevant for the purposes of this book is the fact that the work of people involved in Ankarana's sapphire and ecotourist trades supplies the demands of foreign consumers.

Search: Global Bazaar

Googling the phrase "global bazaar" will take you shopping. The first link that comes up when I search these terms brings me to a site advertising a recent tradeshow in New York City organized by *Travel and Leisure* magazine (*Travel and Leisure* 2011). At the 2011 occurrence of this event, *Travel and Leisure*'s readers were offered the opportunity to "explore the global bazaar": to "taste the famed street foods of Singapore," for example, and to see "Bula dancers from Fiji." Attendees were also given the chance to consider the possibilities presented by different vacation destinations, everything from the "singular natural wonders" of South Africa to the "cultural richness and striking natural beauty" of Chile, and to browse the "authentic goods" offered by a range of retailers. One vendor in this "global bazaar" scours the earth "for exotic, exclusive, and edgy finds from the world's most stylish destinations," for example, while another offers "exotic essentials for the home and garden" from Marrakesh.

Surely this isn't the global bazaar I refer to in the subtitle of this book? In a sense, it is. As I have come to understand it through the research documented here, the global economy in which people involved in Ankarana's sapphire and ecotourist trades have become caught up is perhaps better known to foreign consumers as a system that presents them with a world of "transporting," "sensuous," and "authentic" commodities and experiences akin to those on offer at the event described above.

My interest in the global systems and processes that have given rise to Ankarana's sapphire and ecotourist trades was first sparked by questions and speculations of the sort mentioned earlier: questions about the future uses of sapphires, for example, and about the *real* intentions of foreign visitors to the region (Walsh 2004, 2005). Sitting at the roadside in Ambondromifehy, watching as kilograms of sapphires were leaving Ankarana while truckloads of ecotourists were arriving, it was hard *not* to wonder, as the people with whom I was sitting did, at the paradoxes presented by a humming global economy in a place like this. People and commodities were coming and going, and plenty of money was being made from all of this activity, but who was really benefitting? More precisely, who was benefitting most, how were they managing to do so, and at what cost to others? It was hard to conceive of Malagasy sapphire miners who risked being killed by cave-ins or arrested inside Ankarana National Park as winners in all this, or to imagine that Malagasy sapphire traders being cheated by their foreign counterparts were flourishing competitors on what some claim is a level global economic playing field (Friedman 2005; see also Aronica and Ramdoo 2006). Just down the road, in Mahamasina, the scene was just as perplexing. Here, several dozen Malagasy people were doing quite well from hosting and guiding foreign visitors to Ankarana National Park, but several hundred others living within a short walk of the park entrance experienced the burdens and surveillance that came with conservation efforts much more than they did the benefits of ecotourism. There was no doubt that wealthy foreign visitors were *attracted* to Ankarana National Park's undisturbed ecosystems—but where were the opportunities that were meant to come *with* them?

My decision to use the phrase "global bazaar" to refer to what I saw of the global economy's workings in Ankarana is more than a product of my dissatisfaction with other, more popular and googlable, metaphors. My use of this phrase was inspired, rather, by how people in Ankarana have come to experience and understand the global economy themselves through their work in and observations of the region's sapphire and ecotourist trades. As discussed in Chapter 2, both Ambondromifehy's sapphire trade and its global counterpart share certain features of the Moroccan *suq*, or bazaar, described by Geertz (1979). As Geertz envisioned it, a bazaar economy is an economic system that involves participants not just in the buying, selling, and trading that one would expect to find in any market, but also in a perpetual "search for information" (1979: 124) that will help them get ahead. Like Geertz's bazaar, Ankarana's sapphire trade is a context in which good information (on matters ranging from the qualities of sapphires to the state of the global market for these stones) is "intensely valued" (1979: 124) but hard to find, and, as in any bazaar economy, this makes those who are less informed especially vulnerable in dealings with those who know more. Indeed for players in Ankarana's sapphire bazaar, as for the participants in Geertz's bazaar, the primary problem encountered is "not balancing options but finding out what they are" (1979: 125). Not only do Ambondromifehy's miners and traders know what they don't, and can't, know about the workings of the global bazaar in which they have become caught up, they know how much this stands to hurt them.

As my research interests expanded beyond Ambondromifehy to include Ankarana's ecotourist trade and, eventually, the global industries that make marketable commodities of the region's sapphires and ecotourist attractions, the image of the global bazaar came to seem even more appropriate. Viewed from away, Ankarana is clearly a source of one-of-a-kind natural wonders: "natural" sapphires that have taken shape in the ground here over millions of years, for example; and "natural" areas featuring Madagascar's famed endemic biodiversity. Ultimately, though, the full economic value of these natural wonders can only ever be realized by drawing them into a global bazaar that is not so different from the one put on by *Travel and Leisure* magazine—that is, a marketplace in which foreign consumers can browse a world of one-of-a-kind options that are, in fact, all of a very similar kind. Simply put, the global bazaar that I intend to describe in this book is one that presents a world of paradoxes to people in Ankarana while presenting a world of possibilities to foreign browsers.

As demonstrated throughout this Introduction, browsing the global bazaar has never been easier for many people in the world—if you are reading these words, you are probably no more than a few search terms away from more information than you could ever want about Madagascar, Ankarana, sapphires, and ecotourism. As you may also have gathered by now, however, having access to an engine designed to facilitate "the search for information" (Geertz 1979) that so occupies people in any bazaar economy is no guarantee of being able to process search results in meaningful ways. In fact, the Internet is as much a feature of the global bazaar described in this book as it is a tool that we might use to try to understand it. Like the "enormously complicated, poorly articulated, and extremely noisy communication networks" (1979: 125) that connect people in Geertz's bazaar, the Internet can give the global bazaar the feel of something knowable. Indeed, Geertz's description of the bazaar as a "crowd of rivals, a clatter of words, and a vast collection of ponderable news" (1979: 203) may serve just as well to describe what Internet searches of the sort described in the previous pages can provide. "Pondering" all this news "and coming to decisions about what to make of it" is no easy task, however; "keeping your feet" on the Internet, as in Geertz's "bazaar mob," "is mainly a matter of deciding whom, what, and how much to believe" (1979: 203).

This book does not argue for or against the value of the Internet, nor is it intended as a consumer's guide to the global bazaar. It is, rather, a work of anthropology that, like others of its kind, has come from a distinctive kind of search for information on the people, places, and processes introduced in the preceding pages.

Search: Madagascar and Anthropology

Searching the terms "Madagascar and anthropology" through Google's "scholar" portal will tell you as much about anthropology as it will about what anthropologists have made of, and in, Madagascar over the years. Some of the links that appear will lead you to the products of "social" or "cultural" anthropological research focusing on living Malagasy people and communities. Others will lead you to the work of "physical" or "biological" anthropologists and primatologists whose research focuses mostly on Madagascar's other, non-human, primate inhabitants—the 35 species of lemurs that call the island home. Still more links will lead you to the work of linguistic anthropologists who have studied the development and use of the Malagasy language, and to the work of archaeologists who have studied human settlement and state formation in Madagascar. It isn't only anglophones who are interested in the anthropology of Madagascar, however. Searching "Madagascar et Anthropologie" from Google's French homepage will net you an equally varied list of sources from francophone anthropologists, many of them Malagasy. Although most of the sources that come up in such searches might be classified as anthropological, the scholarly traditions underlying the approaches to the study of humanity on which they are based are often very different. This same observation applies to this book, as well. The approach that I have taken in my own "search for information" on the topics addressed in the chapters that follow is one I have learned.

What first drew me to anthropology as an undergraduate student was the great ambition of the discipline. The class that hooked me was one in which I had to read what seemed like an odd assortment of things: a classic article concerning the relationships between mothers' brothers and sisters' sons in southern Africa (Radcliffe-Brown 1952), for example, as well as a more recent paper about the meaning of professional wrestling matches in small-town Ontario (Freedman 1983), and *Germinal*, Emile Zola's fictional account of life in a nineteenth-century French coal-mining town. These sources, and others like them, made a simple point in necessarily complex ways: all people everywhere lead complicated but not incomprehensible lives. Tutorial discussions of the ethnographic research methods behind these sources made sense to me: If you want to know more about how people think about and act in the world, then you must take the time it needs to ask them good questions and to understand the answers. Live, talk, sit, walk, and eat with people. Listen more than you speak. Pay attention. Get involved when you can. Although anthropologists (and others who take this approach) are destined to consult a wide range of sources in order to better understand the systemic features of, and broader influences on, social life that are often hard to discern in the midst of it, the kind of anthropology that drew me to the discipline was fundamentally grounded in the idea of "taking people seriously" (MacClancy 2002a) in the way that one takes any partner in a meaningful conversation seriously.

Taking people seriously in the way that anthropology encourages can lead to approaches and careers that some might consider unconventional. This book, for example, is based not simply on dozens of hours of recorded interviews (some of which will be quoted directly in the chapters that follow), but on hundreds of hours spent in conversation, and hundreds of days spent living, with people in Ankarana. Sometimes, conversations took place at "social locations" (Cerwonka and Malkki 2007: 50)—in trading booths by the side of the road in Ambondromifehy, for example, or on a bench in Mahamasina at which Malagasy guides would gather to wait for foreign clients. Other times, these conversations involved spending time with people on the move—with mobile traders heading into Ankarana National Park to buy sapphires from miners, for example, and with foreign ecotourists touring the park. As often happens in this sort of research, these conversations have tended to direct my interests as much as they have served them. Although anthropological researchers always bring their own peculiar aspirations and the baggage of their training with them, so long as their research involves listening to people with different priorities, it is hard to stay on a pre-determined course. This is not a drawback of the discipline, mind you. When taking people seriously is more than just a method—when it inspires research rather than just enables it—the topics it leads to are always worth considering.

People involved in Ankarana's sapphire trade are among millions in the world who live in the wake of internationally traded commodities, working to supply the demand of distant, and often unknown, markets. In fact, this book joins others in the genre of anthropological writing that has emerged in recent decades to describe how some of the world's most marginal workers are connected to distant consumers through, for example, the tomatoes they pick on Mexican farms (Barndt 2002), the broccoli they grow in Guatemalan fields (Fischer and Benson 2006), or, in an especially influential historical case study, the sugar cane they cut on Caribbean plantations (Mintz 1985). In Chapters 2 and 4, I show how similar commodity connections might be drawn through a consideration of the international trade of Ankarana's sapphires.

As noted earlier, a significant feature of sapphire work in Ankarana is that it often involves extracting and/or trading gemstones that are obtained illegally from within the boundaries of a nearby National Park; as signs posted all around the park make clear, this place is meant to be off-limits to miners. As you might imagine, though, the reasoning behind such restrictions makes more sense to those who would like to conserve Ankarana's biodiversity than it does to those looking to extract what might be sold from this place. This situation is not so unusual; similar conflicts of interest have been studied in conservation hotspots around the world (see, for example, Igoe 2004, West 2006, and Vivanco 2007, for example). In Madagascar specifically, such research has been especially good at pointing out the problems that come with placing the bulk of the burden of conserving the world's endangered species and ecosystems on the shoulders of those who are least able to bear it (see Harper 2002, Keller 2008, and Sodikoff 2009, for example). In Chapter 3, I continue in this tradition of research, pointing out the limits and complications that can come with promoting ecotourism, in particular, as a means for achieving conservation and development goals simultaneously.

Based on my description of what is to come in the following chapters, some might imagine that this book is about two very different topics: Ankarana's sapphire trade, on the one hand, and the region's ecotourist trade, on the other. In fact, there is good reason to consider these trades alongside one another as I do here. What became clear to me while shuttling between Ambondromifehy and Mahamasina over the past decade is something that Ankarana's speculators had assumed all along: namely, that these two trades are not nearly as different or disconnected as some might assume. As I discuss in Chapter 4, they are fundamentally similar, for example, in how they supply foreign demand for what I term "natural wonders"—dazzling gemstones and awe-inspiring ecotourist attractions that are commoditized and valued in ways that reveal just how profoundly entangled foreign consumers are in the global bazaar that people in Ankarana have come to know through a very different sort of experience. In sum, my goal is to show you that the global bazaar seen from a roadside in Ankarana is the same one you might see from an entrance to the aforementioned trade show in New York City, or from an Internet search of "sapphires" or "ecotourism," or even, as I will discuss in the first half of the Conclusion, from a seat at a table in a Starbucks around the corner. You can't get away from it. Indeed, as I discuss in the second half of the Conclusion, even this book can be understood as a product of many of the global systems and processes that it claims to be about.

Welcome to the bazaar.

THE PLACE OF THE ROCKS

During my first stay in the Ankarana region of northern Madagascar—"the place of the rocks"—I lived in a small village located approximately five kilometres to the west of the Ankarana massif. Around three months after arriving, I went to visit an elderly neighbour whom I had come to know as Dadilahy or "grandfather"—a man who was widely recognized as an authority on the history of Ankarana, and thus someone from whom I had a great deal to learn. As I often did on visits like this, I brought a detailed map of the region with me, hoping that as Dadilahy recounted the comings and goings of the past several centuries, I might be able to keep track of where, exactly, the people he was talking about were coming from and going to.

Dadilahy was already speaking with a visitor when I arrived, but he welcomed me anyhow and had me sit. Eventually, conversation turned to my presence in the village and, then, to the map rolled up in my hand. I explained to my fellow visitor, as I had just recently learned to do in the Malagasy language, that I had come to Ankarana to "learn stories" about this place and the people who live here. Unrolling the map brought the reaction I had come to expect. My fellow visitor marvelled, remarking that he had never seen such a detailed depiction of the region and "the rocks" at its centre. When he wondered aloud as to why such a map had ever been produced, Dadilahy replied before I could, telling both of us that foreigners, or *vazaha* as they are commonly known in Madagascar, have maps like this because of the special interest they take in places like Ankarana. And they are interested in places like Ankarana, he continued, because, where they are from, they've never had, or no longer have, what can be found in such places.

The "rocks" of the Ankarana massif.
Photo by Emma Hunter.

Dadilahy's observations, I soon learned, were drawn from a lifetime of observing *vazaha* like me—foreigners stumbling around the region with notebooks, cameras, and poorly translated explanations of what we were doing here. As indicated most obviously by the maps we brought with us, foreigners knew and thought about Ankarana quite differently than local people did. That these maps were created at all was a clear indication of our desire to record aspects of the place that were imperceptible from the ground; that these maps were mass-produced and widely circulated indicated our desire to communicate to like-minded others what we had learned. It didn't matter to Dadilahy that the map I had brought with me on that day was, in fact, produced by Madagascar's own topographical service. As a local historian, he understood that this way of representing the region was not of local origin. He also understood that, as with all maps, this one revealed just as much about the people who made it and find it useful as it did about the place depicted. Foreigners have always considered Ankarana to be a source of something that can't be found elsewhere, he contended. This is why they have created such detailed records of the place, and this is why they keep coming back.

The local history I learned from Dadilahy over the years I knew him revealed that "the rocks" of Ankarana were important to people long before anyone thought to put them on a map. Indeed, for him and many others who call themselves "Antankarana," or the "people of the place of the rocks," the Ankarana massif was, and remains, a kind of place that a map can't describe—a site of shared history, memories, and ceremonies, and, as such, a sacred place that must be carefully managed if it is to go on providing the unifying and sustaining force that many seek in it. In recent decades, local traditional authorities have found allies among conservationists who would also like to see Ankarana protected, though for reasons of their own. As conservation agencies and organizations see it, the Ankarana massif figures at the centre of an ecosystem unlike any in the world; it is a natural wonder that must be protected lest it be destroyed by the people who live around it. And as far as these observers are concerned, the people who pose the biggest threat to Ankarana's precious biodiversity are those who have come to see the massif and its surrounding forests as places of opportunity—places in which sapphires and other valuable natural resources might be found and extracted.

In the next three sections, I discuss three different ways of thinking about what makes Ankarana special. If we are interested in learning more about "the place of the rocks," then we ought to begin by considering the perspectives of others whose interests in the region are already well established. As should become clear as I proceed, however, none of these perspectives is broad enough on its own to reveal what makes Ankarana so special for the purposes of this book. In fact, as I will point out in the conclusion to the chapter, what makes Ankarana special to me is that it is a place in which such different perspectives have been drawn together, and knotted up, in ways that can tell us something important about the complexities of the wider world. Let me begin, though, as Dadilahy would, with the "people of the place of the rocks" and what makes Ankarana special to them.

Ankarana as a Sacred Place

The word "Antankarana" is one of many ethnic terms in Madagascar that suggests a connection between a particular group of people and a particular landscape. We must be careful, however, not to presume too much of a connection like this. Although everyone I know who considers themselves to be Antankarana recognizes the significance of "the rocks" from which this term originates, not everyone who lives in and around the Ankarana massif today considers themselves to be Antankarana. And so it has been from early on. According to Dadilahy, the only affiliations that mattered to the very first residents of Ankarana were those that connected them to others with whom they were related through descent or marriage. It wasn't until the region's diverse and dispersed population united in common support of a newly arrived royal family in the seventeenth century that the possibility of an overarching, region-wide affiliation appeared. The leader of this family and his successors took on the role of *ampanjaka*—or "rulers"—in the region, and the political-religious system that developed around these rulers might be termed a "kingdom."

The connection between the Antankarana kingdom and Ankarana itself is thoroughly rooted in the local landscape. Indeed, whenever Dadilahy told stories of the kingdom's history, he would indicate the places in which these events had taken place, not through reference to a map, as I might have hoped, but by pointing his knuckle or chin in one direction or another. Over the years I knew him, I witnessed him tell these stories many times. The Ankarana massif, he would say, pointing eastward from his home village, is where rulers, their families, and their followers took refuge when armies of other Malagasy groups invaded the region. While hiding in the massif's caves, he would continue in the most commonly repeated of these stories, one nineteenth-century ruler named Tsimiharo sought the advice of a young sorceress who directed him to lead his followers out of the massif, westward to the nearby coast, and on, by boat, still farther westward to the small island of Nosy Mitsio. There, Dadilahy continued, Tsimiharo sought out allies who could help him return to the mainland, eventually forging an alliance with the *vazaha*—the French, in this case—with whose help Tsimiharo's descendants eventually reinstalled themselves here, in *this* place. The landscape covered in Dadilahy's stories of eighteenth- and nineteenth-century events was never the landscape of a distant past; it was an immediate landscape, known to audiences and their ancestors through experience.

As mentioned in the Introduction, I first entered the Ankarana massif in 1992 while participating in an Antankarana ceremony known as the "entry into the caves." It began on a Thursday with the establishment of a large camp on the western edge of the massif. Here, hundreds of people from throughout the region gathered, bringing enough rice, cattle, and other provisions to last us through the three days we would be there. It rained the first night—a good omen, I was told, given that one of the purposes of our visits was to ensure a good rice harvest for the following year. The discomfort of the mud that came with the rain was all part of the event—"if you don't suffer a little," I was told, "what good will come of it?" We spent most of the next two days scrambling barefoot around the edges of the massif, making our way over outcrops of sharp limestone and into the serpentine caves that would lead us to the tombs of past rulers that were our destinations.

We opened and drank the gourds of honey mead that had been brought to these sites as offerings five years earlier, and replaced them with new ones that would be drunk five years hence. We were in the midst of a cycle. Participants' connection to these sites had both a past and a future. It was a connection that people say should, and will, "never die."

At times, it seemed as though our entry into the caves was meant to be commemorative; many of the stories told, songs sung, and dances performed over those few days recalled past events. Here was the sunken forest in which Tsimiharo and his followers found sustenance; there was the escape passage to which the sorceress led them. In truth, however, we were doing what we were doing for the sake of the future. The explicit goals of each day's visits were realized only when the living ruler invoked his ancestors at each site, informed them of what was happening in the world they left behind, and requested "blessing" (Bloch 1986) and the rains and good harvests it would bring to everyone in the region. He was not the only one to seek blessing at these sites, however. Others in our party lined up to make requests, too, intent on receiving blessing for projects of their own. Some wanted more children or grandchildren; others wanted more cattle. In all cases, the blessing sought was something that, like the rain sought by the ruler, was deemed necessary for the future.

What I was witnessing during that first visit to the Ankarana massif in 1992 was a manifestation of what Keller terms "the Malagasy ethos of growth" (Keller 2008: 652)—a lived philosophy based on "the ideal of the fruitful continuation and growth of human life" (651). The ruler's followers did not accompany him into these caves out of blind devotion. They did so, rather, in search of the sacred force of which he and his ancestors were conduits—a force with the power to enable prosperity, fertility, good health, and other features of life that are essential to growth. With the stakes so high, these pilgrims had to be careful. Throughout Madagascar, sacred sites at which blessing might be sought are not just powerful and attractive; they are also fragile places that need tending to (see, for example, Middleton 1999).

Over those few days in and around the Ankarana massif in 1992, there was much discussion of customs (*fomba*) that had to be followed and taboos (*fady*) that had to be respected. I scribbled madly. The tombs had to be visited in a certain order. Women had to untie their braided hair while men had to work four braids into theirs. Flashlights were forbidden, and so on. In retrospect, I realize that in my anxiety over making sure that I was getting all of these facts down, I lost sight of just how anxious these details were making many of those around me. For my fellow pilgrims, getting things right was more than just a matter of following rules: getting things right was necessary to achieving the goal of our visits; getting things wrong, on the other hand, might mean more troubling possibilities. Transgressing a taboo, for example, could result in a scorpion bite for a transgressor or illness befalling a transgressor's child. Using a flashlight instead of the prescribed palm-leaf torch might get you lost in a cave.

Mention of living rulers, ancestral rulers, and pilgrims in search of blessing might lead some to imagine that the Antankarana kingdom must be structured something like a pyramid, with royalty firmly positioned at the top and their followers arrayed beneath them, holding them up. In fact, it is much more complicated than that. As I came to understand it, the Antankarana kingdom might be more appropriately described as being like an hourglass. It is a system in which the living ruler finds himself precariously positioned at the narrow neck that separates demanding ancestors above him and demanding followers beneath. This position is a powerful one, to be sure, but it isn't always enviable. In fact, few are more constrained by customs and taboos than the living ruler himself. If he is to remain the conduit through which his ancestors and his followers pass what is theirs to give, he must be protected. He must not be touched or even talked about in certain ways, for example, nor is he meant to eat his meals with others or from just any plate. Such taboos are burdensome to more than just the ruler, however. People who consider their own well-being to be bound up with that of the living ruler are his most vigilant protectors. For these followers, greeting the ruler with a prescribed expression of devotion is not simply an indication of subservience in the face of power. In not taking his hand in theirs, as they might when greeting someone else, followers mark the ruler off as someone fragile and in need of protection—someone who must be approached very carefully lest the powerful and potentially productive sacred force he embodies be made inaccessible.

I mention all this because Antankarana people relate to *places* associated with past rulers in much the same way as they do with the living ruler himself—these places might also be understood as occupying the essential but fragile neck of an hourglass. The tombs of past rulers inside the massif are points of access to a force that can help those who are drawn to them to make the most of their lives in the region, and as such they are very special places that must be protected. Just as the living ruler is threatened by the inattention of those around him, sites like these tombs can be rendered ineffective by the disrespect of those they attract. When the taboos that are meant to regulate people's behaviour around these sites *are* transgressed, it is the sites themselves, and not the taboos, that are liable to be spoken of as having been "broken". No wonder the pilgrims with whom I visited these sites in 1992 were so anxious about getting things right.

With all of this in mind, some might assume that outsiders would not be welcome during these visits. This is not the case. I wasn't even the only foreign anthropologist present at the events described above—Lisa Gezon, a fellow researcher, participated in all of these visits as well. Also present at various times over those few days were politicians, TV news reporters, representatives of the French consulate, French tourists, and representatives of the World Wildlife Fund, the international conservation organization that had just recently assumed responsibility for managing the conservation area that encompasses the Ankarana massif.

All of us outsiders had been invited to attend by the living ruler, Tsimiharo III, a man who never shied away from an opportunity to let the country and the world know of the vitality of the Antankarana kingdom. He understood that the sacred sites within the massif and the ritual visits that brought people to them carried great symbolic weight for outsiders. No one who visited the forest campsite and saw pilgrims celebrating through the rainy night could doubt the ruler's ability to marshal supporters around him; and no one who negotiated the massif's dark passages alongside these followers (barefoot, and by torch-light) could fail to recognize the depth of their devotion to the sacred force that could be accessed in this place.

As Gezon (1997, 2006) has argued in her own account of the visit just described, the presence of such different players in this special place was a sure sign of the complexity of the situation we shared. Consider, for example, that the campsite in which we were spending our nights and the caves into which we were travelling during the day were located inside a "protected area" that fell under the authority of the World Wildlife Fund (WWF), and that our stay thus involved the violation of several conservation rules that were in force at the time (Gezon 1997: 91). Consider too, that the ruler did not ask for permission from these conservation agencies to host this event. Instead, *he* invited *them* to attend. And he did so to make a point. "The people from WWF never used to believe that the forest belongs to me and my ancestors," the ruler told Gezon, "but they believe it now." (Gezon 2006: 164). But why did these conservationists come when invited on this unsanctioned visit to the place they were meant to be protecting? Why, for that matter, were they intent on protecting this place at all? The best way to answer these questions is to consider another way in which Ankarana has been considered special over the years.

According to the editors of a *Reader's Digest* encyclopedia that I received on my thirteenth birthday, Ankarana is among the "Natural Wonders of the World." In this source, however, the story of the place is nothing like the one I heard from Dadilahy. Ankarana, we are told here, is

> composed of 150-million-year-old limestone, soft and chalky in the upper part, hard and crystalline at the base. ... In those places where the crystalline limestone has been stripped of its chalky cover, the bare surface has been dissolved into a pattern of channels and ridges called lapis by geologists and known locally as *tsingy.* ... Bristling with jagged ridges, sharp pinnacles and knifelike blades, these areas are impassable to anyone traveling on foot. (Scheffel and Wernert 1980: 48)

This description took me aback when I read it in 1993, fresh back in Canada from my first visit to Ankarana. I had opened this book in the hope of finding something familiar. Instead, I found the place that I had come to know in the previous months described as "impassable." "Only from a plane or a helicopter," this source suggested, "is it possible to appreciate the grandeur of this spectacular karst landscape" (1980: 48). Absent was any discussion of the rich human history of the massif, or of the sacred sites I had just recently visited.

The image of Ankarana as a natural wonder goes back to the earliest European accounts of the place. In an 1877 article, for example, Batchelor, a touring Anglican missionary, described the massif as "an enormous lofty precipitous rock" (Batchelor and Kestell-Cornish 1877: 27) that is "one of the most wonderful places to be seen in Madagascar." This reputation only grew through the twentieth century with reports from French administrators who were posted in the region following France's colonization of the island in 1896. Word went out about all there was to be seen in Ankarana, as well as the opportunities that its forests and rivers offered foreign hunters to "satisfy their passion for [shooting] crocodiles, wood ducks, wild pigs and birds" (Sauphanor 1939: 19). Many elders in the region remember well how French administrators and settlers from the nearby town of Ambilobe would drive to the massif in their trucks for picnics, eating and drinking in the cool sand at one or another of the massif's dramatic cave entrances, hunting while there, and then leaving leftover loaves of bread with village children on their way home. To these foreign explorers, picnickers, and hunters, the massif was not a place of tombs, pilgrimages or shared history. It was, rather, a place to discover, a place for scenic Sunday excursions, and, as Batchelor put it, a "place that would well repay being further investigated" (1877: 27). By the 1950s, it was also deemed to be a place special enough to warrant a particular kind of protection.

As suggested in the previous section, Antankarana rulers had developed close relations with the French since the mid-nineteenth century. Indeed, these rulers often made public declarations of their support for the French at events like the cave-tomb visits just described—events to which French settlers and administrators were invited during the colonial era in much the same way that foreign researchers, tourists, and representatives of conservation organizations are invited today (Walsh 2001b). Not surprisingly, then, when the French created the Réserve Spéciale d'Ankarana (the Ankarana Special Reserve) in 1956, they did so with the support of the Antankarana ruler of the time.

As far as people in Ankarana are concerned, present-day foreigners who visit what has since been renamed Ankarana National Park share a good deal in common with the foreign explorers, hunters, and picnickers of the past. It would be a mistake, however, to trivialize the amount of work that foreign and Malagasy scientists have put into establishing the international reputation of this place as more than just a site of nice views and picnic spots. In a recent summary of this research, Cardiff and Befourouack suggest that "[n]owhere else in the world can one find Ankarana's combination of pinnacle karst [limestone formations], caves, underground rivers and isolated sunken forests" (2003: 1501). This conservation area, they continue, features "more than 111 km of caves" (1502), "at least 330 species of plants" (1504), "at least 60 species of reptiles and amphibians" (1504), "at least 89 species of birds" (1504), and "at least one species of mammal known only from the reserve" (1504), a mouse lemur that has only recently been described in the scientific literature. And research has only just begun; the full range of Ankarana's "unique set of habitats and community of endemic organisms" (1503) has yet to be documented. Time is of the essence, however. Cardiff and Befourouack end their overview of Ankarana's "unique fauna and flora" with a discussion of "new and old threats to [their] conservation" (1505).

Part of what makes Ankarana so special to some observers is the fact that its distinctive biodiversity is perceived to be under threat, and as conservationists see it, the biggest threats facing Ankarana National Park are anthropogenic, originating with the behaviour of people who live alongside of and among all of the biodiversity listed above. It bears noting, however, that

A habituated golden-crowned lemur inside Ankarana National Park.

these anthropogenic threats are not new to the region. The main path that runs through the middle of Ankarana National Park today originated during the 1940s and 1950s as a logging road (Cardiff and Befourouack 2003: 1506), and much of the original forest to the south of the park was to agriculture lost with the introduction of exportable cash crops like cotton and sugar cane during the colonial era. Even hunting, identified by Cardiff and Befourouak as "the greatest threat to crocodiles in Madagascar" (2003: 1506), has a long history; bear in mind that the endangered crocodiles inhabiting Ankarana today are the descendants of those that had been pointed out as potential targets in the earlier-cited account of good hunting spots in the region. In short, it is not the nature of the threats to the region's biodiversity that has changed most dramatically in recent decades, but rather the reactions that such threats have inspired, from concerned outsiders especially.

International interest in protecting Ankarana's threatened biodiversity boomed in the late 1980s and early 1990s with, among other things, the publication of several accounts of the biodiversity of this "rediscovered nature reserve" (Wilson, Stewart, and Fowler 1988), and the production of several popular nature documentaries concerning the place. Within the region itself, meanwhile, the implementation of Madagascar's National Environmental Action Plan (NEAP) during the 1990s, to be discussed further in Chapter 3, made unprecedented resources available for promoting the cause of conservation. While living in Ankarana during this time, I saw the effects of all this attention. Public meetings were held in villages surrounding the massif to inform residents of the goals of conservation projects being undertaken in their midst. Several young men I knew were hired to serve as reserve guards, while others received training and certification to work as guides. Schoolchildren were given glossy colour textbooks that taught (in the local dialect of Malagasy) not just about the region's biodiversity but also about the customs and taboos that are meant to regulate people's relationships with the land. A local pop singer, Mily Clement, had a huge radio hit with a conservation-themed song called "Spitting while lying on your back." "Don't burn the brush to make new rice-fields, brother-in-law," he sang, "don't kill animals indiscriminately," repeating over and over again the key argument of the conservation cause: unsustainable practices like these will only get *you* in the end, like spitting up in the air while lying on your back.

The early 1990s were also a time when foreign and Malagasy representatives of the World Wildlife Fund and its partner Malagasy agency went out of their way to try to engage and win the support of local traditional authorities. Getting influential people such as the Antankarana ruler to champion conservation, planners hoped, could do a great deal to sway others in the region. And so it was that whenever they were invited by the ruler to attend events like the ceremony discussed in the previous section, representatives of the WWF not only accepted but gave their support. In doing so, they acknowledged the special connection that exists between the massif and the local people who took their name from it. Accordingly, today's visitors to Ankarana National Park are expected to follow a list of rules that include not only the prohibitions that one would expect to be in effect in any conservation area, but also a list of specific taboos insisted upon by the Antankarana ruler and his followers. Thus, not only are visitors not meant to feed the lemurs or leave garbage behind, but they are also prohibited, in accordance with Antankarana custom, from whistling or bringing pork inside the caves of the massif. In return for such recognition, the ruler has often reciprocated with support of his own. At a ceremony marking the fortieth anniversary of the creation of the Ankarana Special Reserve, for example, he publicly championed the cause of conservation. "The wisdom of my ancestors and the philosophy of conservation are joined as one," he announced to an audience that included Prince Philip, the Duke of Edinburgh, travelling through Madagascar as an ambassador of the WWF. "Having inherited this philosophy," he continued, "I wish to reiterate that the Gods and our ancestors have supported, are supporting and will always support us in the noble cause [i.e., environmental conservation] that we defend for the good of our descendents."

Careful readers may note a similarity between this recent ruler's support for the "noble cause" of conservation and his predecessors' support of the French during colonial times. Just as rulers of the colonial era made the most of their special relationships with the French to negotiate benefits for family members and followers, so has their successor been adamant that Antankarana people must get something out of the interest that conservationists have taken in the region. He has lobbied for Antankarana people to be hired as guards and to be trained as guides, for example, and has been unwavering in his stance that intensified attempts at conserving Ankarana's biodiversity should not interfere with local residents' access to the cave-tombs and other sacred sites located within the protected area's boundaries. And just as the French made useful allies out of Antankarana rulers throughout the colonial era, international conservation organizations and national conservation agencies have gone out of their way to include the current ruler in their plans (Gezon 2006).

The scenario described in both this section and the last would seem to hold out the possibility of producing winners all around—protecting what is special about Ankarana is clearly something that many of the players I have been describing thus far want to do. This scenario may also seem quite familiar to some readers: the great potential represented by the apparent confluence of interests of conservationists and indigenous groups have made similar scenarios common in conservation hot spots around the world in recent decades (Brockington, Duffy, and Igoe 2008). Time has tended to show that such scenarios are never as simple as they seem, however. In Ankarana, as in other parts of the world, traditional leaders who claim, or are considered by others, to have authority over large groups of people don't always have the kind of influence that they or others hope they do— especially not when they appear to privilege the interests of outsiders over those of the people for whom they claim to speak (Gezon 1997; see also, for example, Conklin and Graham 1995). Conservationists, meanwhile, often operate with a selective and, thus, incomplete vision of the lives and traditions of the "local people" with whom they seek to ally themselves, celebrating certain aspects of indigenous culture that appear to fall in line with the goals of conservation, while ignoring or even disparaging others that may work against these goals (see, for example, Keller 2008, 2009). And then there is everyone else: the many more thousands of people who actually live in and around places deemed to be in need of conservation—people whose needs and motivations are far more complicated than any number of public meetings, glossy textbooks or pop songs could ever hope to address.

The pilgrims with whom I visited the tombs of past rulers inside the Ankarana massif in 1992 were not intent on protecting these sites for the sake of conserving the endemic biodiversity that could be found in the caves, rivers, and forests around them. For them, moderating and monitoring behaviour around the massif's sacred sites was more a matter of protecting these places as sources of the blessing that they hoped would bring prosperity, fertility, and health to people living in the region. As noted in the previous section, their efforts at protecting what is special about Ankarana were rooted in an "ethos of growth" (Keller 2008). Think for a moment, however, about what this all-important growth is meant to bring to them. For those who seek access to blessing inside the massif, success will be measured in new births, expanding herds, and increasing yields of rice and cash-crops; the growth they desire will come to the local landscape in the form of new and bigger houses, more grazing cattle, and fields of newly planted sugar cane. As you might imagine, indications of growth such as these would *not* be signs of success to those whose goal is protecting Ankarana's distinctive biodiversity; in fact, the work of conservation is founded in an ethos that lends itself to quite dissimilar aspirations. As Keller puts it, "the conservationist ethos" is one founded on the ideal of maintaining "equilibrium among the different species present on the planet" (2008: 251). And when the "protection of biodiversity and the conservation of the present state of things" (653) is the goal, the kind of growth ensured by sacred sites like those to be found within the Ankarana massif will always represent a problem.

Population growth is often identified as an especially great threat to endangered biodiversity in conservation hotspots. The more people one finds living around protected areas like Ankarana National Park, the greater the likelihood of anthropogenic threats. Thus in Madagascar, which has seen significant population growth in recent decades, conservationists have concerned themselves both with monitoring the effects of population growth around protected areas and with family-planning programs through which such growth might be stemmed. There are some kinds of growth that no amount of monitoring or family planning can regulate, however. In Ankarana, for example, the population growth that has been seen as most threatening by conservationists over the past 20 years has been caused by the immigration of Malagasy people from outside the region who have come to see Ankarana as neither sacred nor a natural wonder, but as a place of opportunity.

Ankarana as a Place of Opportunity

In this section I introduce a third way of thinking about what makes Ankarana special. In addition to attracting pilgrims, scientists, conservationists, and ecotourists, Ankarana is a place that has long drawn in outsiders who hope to take something more than just blessing, research findings or photographs away with them when they leave.

One way of thinking about the human history of Ankarana is in terms of the many arrivals that have made this region what it is today. As noted earlier, the region's earliest settlers witnessed the arrival of royalty who, in turn, saw the arrival of Malagasy enemies and French allies. The colonial era (1896–1960) brought European settlers, and with them plantations of sugar cane, coconut palm, cotton, and other exportable cash crops; not far away, to the east of the French administrative centre of Ambilobe, a gold mine was established as well. Colonial-era projects such as these needed more labour than the existing, Antankarana population could provide, however, and so migrants from other parts of Madagascar filled the void. Some of these twentieth-century Malagasy immigrants settled into existing communities, adopting the customs, taboos, and livelihoods of their Antankarana neighbours (Gezon 2006). Others brought customs, taboos, and specialties of their own, maintaining connections with the places in Madagascar from which they had come with the intention of an eventual return. As far as conservationists are concerned, however, none of these past arrivals can compare with the flood of new arrivals brought in by the sapphire rush that gripped the region in 1996.

The vanguard of Ankarana's sapphire rush consisted of Malagasy and foreign prospectors exploring, staking claims, and then setting up small mechanical mines in the hills to the east of Ankarana National Park. Malagasy migrants with experience in small-scale gold mining followed soon after, working on the margins of these mechanical mines, assuming correctly that sapphires could be found throughout the region. The most daring independent prospectors eventually found the bonanzas they were seeking in caves and forests to the west of the national highway, inside Ankarana National Park. The few guards charged with monitoring the park's eastern boundary were in no position to stop the hundreds—and, by 1997, thousands—of miners who started flooding in, so, eventually, Malagasy police and military were brought in to try to keep miners out. Heightened security did little more than further complicate an already complicated local economy, however. Miners were arrested, sapphires were confiscated, and fines were paid, but as long as foreign buyers were willing to pay so well for the little blue stones to be found within the Park, the mining was not going to stop.

When I passed through Ambondromifehy in 1997, it was a crowded and chaotic boomtown of around 15,000 inhabitants—a far cry from the unremarkable village of 400 that had stood there on a trip two years earlier. Once-unencumbered road shoulders had been taken over by hundreds of trading booths crammed side by side over the kilometre-long stretch

"Sapphires change life!"

of highway that marked the boomtown's social and trading centre. Cattle pens and gardens had been replaced by bars and nightclubs specializing in serving overpriced beer to the town's overwhelmingly young and male population. The community's few long-standing, cement-floored houses had been surrounded by thousands of quickly built huts and other temporary structures. The caption on a decorative waistcloth I bought early on in one of the town's hundreds of market stalls said it all: "Sapphires change life!" And not just for those making money from mining and trading these little blue stones: just imagine how life had changed for the 400 long-time residents who had been living here, on their own and undisturbed, only a year earlier.

On my first full day in Ambondromifehy in 1999, I did what any newcomer to a community in the region is meant to do: I sought out local elders—*tompontanana*, people "responsible for the community" (Walsh 2002b)—so that I might introduce myself and explain why I had come. I was led to a cement-floored house 50 metres from the highway, where I introduced myself to a 70-something-year-old man who I would come to call Zama or "uncle", and explained the purpose of my visit. Preliminaries out of the way, conversation turned to the history of this community, and I was able to ask the question that became the focus of my research: What happened here? His answer was one I would hear repeatedly over the ensuing months. It all started with just a few "visitors", he told me: young men from Madagascar's east coast who were as respectful to him as I had been. As they would have been expected to do in any small Malagasy community, they had sought out both him and other long-time residents to inform them of their business here: to look for "stones". In response, Zama welcomed them as he had welcomed me, telling them only that they would have to obey local customs and taboos if they expected to prosper in the region.

By all accounts, the earliest arrivals did as they were told. Some even began calling Zama "grandfather" and asked if he could provide them with the blessing of his own ancestors and local land spirits—blessing that they hoped would help them to succeed in their search for stones. As a good host is meant to do, Zama consented and led a number of these visitors to the base of a tree outside his house, introduced them to the powers he invoked there, and then allowed them access to what he held sacred. In turn, as custom would have it, these prospectors promised to return to this same site with offerings, should they realize the fortunes they were seeking in the region. Zama saw nothing wrong in all this at the start. He and other elders of Ambondromifehy had become accustomed to watching their children and grandchildren leave for opportunities elsewhere, and they were keen on the possibilities for growth represented by the new visitors in their midst.

But the promise of those early days was soon replaced with worry and trouble. As word of the riches to be found in the region spread throughout Madagascar, dozens of new arrivals per week turned to hundreds per day, and the small community that Ambondromifehy had once been was soon enveloped by the chaos of a boom. By the time I sat with Zama in 1999, few newcomers ever approached him to ask permission to settle. Worse yet, some of those who had requested blessing from him and his ancestors in the past had reneged on promises they had made to bring offerings to the tree outside his house. Never again, Zama affirmed. By 1999, he had built a tall fence around the tree. A sacred site at which new arrivals and long-time residents might once have gathered in ways meant to ensure everyone's prosperity and growth had become an endangered site in need of protection from the defiling piss of ignorant and disrespectful visitors.

It bears mentioning here that, like so many people in the region, Zama and other long-time residents of Ambondromifehy were, in fact, relatively new arrivals themselves. The original inhabitants of this settlement had come from the east coast in the early twentieth century to watch over cattle grazing in the region. Seeing it as a place of opportunity, they had stayed, eventually making it unmistakably their own by entombing their dead in nearby caves. These cave-tombs and other newly established sacred places, including the tree outside Zama's house, became sites at which living members of the community could seek blessing that would enable them to realize a prosperous future for themselves and their descendants. Some inhabitants of the town also participated in events associated with the Antankarana kingdom, but for Zama certainly, the sources of blessing that mattered most were to be found in the sacred places that he and his own ancestors had made sacred themselves—the places, like the tree outside his house, that he was inclined to protect for the same reason that Antankarana people are inclined to protect the sacred sites found within the Ankarana massif.

Zama was not the only one concerned about the threats posed by the activities of Ambondromifehy's new arrivals. As noted earlier, miners who had been excluded from private mining operations to the east of the highway were drawn to the sapphires available in caves and forests of Ankarana National Park. In an effort to communicate a clear message to would-be Malagasy-speaking interlopers, managers marked the park's boundaries with signs indicating this conservation area as ALA FADY, a "TABOO FOREST."

Illegal incursions continued regardless, leading conservation evaluators to deem the region's sapphire rush a "total fiasco" (ADAPT 1999: 4). In only two years great damage was reported to have been done to Ankarana's forests; thousands of pits had been dug within Park boundaries, and waterways were silting up as a result of miners sieving and panning sapphires from the clayey dirt these pits produced. In addition, the huge influx of people that the sapphire rush had brought to the region was putting additional pressure on local ecosystems. Miners' shelters and traders' booths had to be made out of something, and, thanks to years of conservation efforts, the nearby "taboo forest" offered the best local supply of

A painted marker of the boundary of Ankarana National Park. In English *ala fady* translates as "taboo forest."

building materials. The park's forests also offered the most convenient local supply of cooking fuel.

Over the months I spent in Ambondromifehy in 1999, I interspersed my visits to Zama with visits to the pits, trading booths, and homes of the new arrivals who were giving long-time residents and conservation workers so much trouble. These visitors had stories of their own to tell: miners told of harrowing passages through the caves of the Ankarana massif and near escapes from the police; novice Malagasy sapphire traders told of being "burned" by the often dishonest foreign buyers to whom they had no choice but to sell their stones; and just about everyone told of fortunes being made and lost through what was called the *biznesy*—the business—of the local sapphire trade. The money earned from sapphires, I often heard, is "hot money"—money that you can't hold on to. And so many of those who had it just spent it, daring to pay the high cost of big bar tabs, road trips, and other distractions that would leave them broke and needing to go out and risk the dangerous work of mining again.

Underlying many of these stories was an ethos that Antankarana pilgrims, conservationists, and Zama himself would all have found troubling. Gone were the deeply embedded place- and kinship-based social networks and the slow and regular patterns of agricultural work that structured life in other communities in the region, replaced by what appeared to be the unstructured, chaotic, "living for the moment" (Day, Papataxiarchis, and Stewart 1999) ethos of a frontier town. Taboo transgressions were commonplace, and many lived in fear of being robbed or cheated by those they had come to trust most. Some new arrivals likened themselves to outlaws, renegades or frontiersmen and their town to the settlements of an imaginary, anarchic, B-movie America. "We live in Los [Angeles]," a miner once told me, invoking the chaotic setting of many of the crime thrillers that were being shown in Ambondromifehy's video parlours. "This place is Texas," noted another young man on another day, calling to mind the frontier of the Westerns of an earlier generation of moviegoers.

During my first stay in Ambondromifehy in 1999, two fires ripped through the town's tightly packed huts, at least ten young men died in mining accidents, and an outbreak of cholera scared many away. As the environmental impact report cited above reported, "the image of Ambondromifehy as an Eldorado" was "giving way to disillusionment with all of the difficulties that miners must ... face" (ADAPT 1999: 9). In fact, by 1999, the boom was already waning. New gemstone rushes in other parts of Madagascar had drawn many foreign buyers and Malagasy prospectors away with the promise of greater fortunes to be made else-where, and within a few years the population of the town was about half of what it had been in the late 1990s. Newcomers continued to arrive through the 2000s, however, a sure sign that even after the rush had ended, Ambondromifehy remained a place of opportunity for some. During visits I made in 2004, 2006, 2008, and 2010, I followed up with people I had met during the early years of the rush, surprised to learn how many of them had stayed on much longer than I or they had ever expected. As these now quite settled visitors saw it, life here after the rush had its advantages. Some of those remaining had taken over the abandoned lots of former neighbours to either expand their own homes or courtyards, or to plant fenced gardens of fruit trees, manioc, and greens. The end of the rush had made Ambondromifehy safer as well. The gangs and thieves that had once terrorized the town were gone, and, as one miner told me in 2008, you can "now sleep with a bag of money as a pillow and not have to worry about it" (Walsh 2012).

What remains most attractive about Ankarana to those who continue to make a living from the local sapphire trade is the National Park itself. Having never been exploited with the industrial machinery employed in the large-scale mining operations found elsewhere in the region, the park remains a place in which miners can still find a steady supply of sapphires. Many have even moved into the park itself, sometimes with their families, to live alongside their pits. Officially their presence here remains illegal, but with the boom long over, little effort is put into keeping them out. And so they will likely stay for the time being. As a miner living inside the park told me in 2010, as long as there are people to buy the sapphires being mined inside Ankarana National Park, there will be people willing to mine them. The opportunities presented by this work may not be what they were at the height of the rush, but they are opportunities nonetheless, and for the people they continue to attract this is clearly enough. One park employee summarized the situation more succinctly than I could ever hope to: "Why do people living around the [National Park] continue to exploit it illegally in the way that they do?" he asked, rhetorically. They do so, he said, because they "would rather die tomorrow than die today."

In the next two chapters, I address the money-making opportunities presented by Ankarana National Park and its resources: first, in the next chapter, the opportunities that have come with the emergence of the region's sapphire trade; and then, in Chapter 3, the opportunities that have come with the emergence of the region's ecotourist trade. Before moving on, though, I want to take one last look at "the place of the rocks," in order to offer some thoughts on what makes this place special to me, at least for the purposes of this book.

What Is So Special about Ankarana?

In the preceding three sections, I have offered three different ways of thinking about what makes Ankarana special—ways of thinking inspired by the perspectives of those who find sacred sites, natural wonders, and opportunities in this place. But what about me, the person whose research produced what you've just read? Surely I must have my own ideas about what makes Ankarana special? I can imagine what Dadilahy must have been thinking when I left the region in 1992, only to return again less than a year later for an even longer stay: If I weren't finding something special in this place—something that I couldn't find anywhere else—why would I keep coming back?

As Dadilahy noted in the story with which I began this chapter, I am certainly not the first researcher to take an interest in what is special about Ankarana. The region's history (Vial 1954, Tsitindry 1987, for example), biodiversity (Wilson, Stewart, and Fowler 1988, Cardiff and Befourouack 2003, for example) and sapphires (Schwarz, Kanis and Schmetzer 2000) have been written about many times before. As you might expect, however, the accounts of Ankarana that have most in common with this one were produced by fellow social scientists (Waast 1973, Theodore 1987, and Jaovelo-Dzao 1996, for example), and of these, the sources alongside which this book fits best are those that focus on how local lives and landscapes have been shaped by what is commonly termed globalization, or *mondialisation* in French (Berger 2012; see also Giguère 2006). As Gezon (2006) puts it, "local landscapes" to the west of Ankarana National Park were "negotiated" and "managed" locally in the face of "global visions" that came to the region with the conservation projects and policies of the 1990s. And as the pitted forests and fields near Ambondromifehy attest, landscapes within and to the east of the park have felt the effects of global demand for gemstones as well. An important part of what makes Ankarana special to me, then, is not what can be found here and nowhere else in the world, but, rather, what can be found here and *everywhere* else. Ankarana is a place in which landscapes, and lives along with them, have been shaped by the current "global situation" (Tsing 2000) that is shared by us all—pilgrims, rulers, conservationists, village elders, miners, jewellery consumers, ecotourists, researchers, and students alike.

If we zoom out from Ankarana, up to a national scale, the region begins to lose some of its distinctiveness. In other parts of Madagascar, where Malagasy people have been engaging with conservation projects and policies while trying to make a living, many of the different perspectives outlined earlier in this chapter can be found coexisting in similarly complex ways (Mulligan 1999, Marcus 2001, and Hanson 2007, for example). If we then zoom out a little more, to a scale encompassing all of Africa, it becomes clear that such complexity is not restricted to Madagascar—indigenous groups, conservationists, miners, and others across the continent also find themselves embroiled in similar conflicts of interest (Brockington 2002, Walley 2004, and Igoe 2004, for example). Zooming out still farther, to the global scale, an even greater distribution of comparable cases is revealed (West 2006 and Vivanco 2007, for example). Some of these many contexts to which Ankarana can be compared are what Tsing calls "zones of awkward engagement" (2005: xi)—that is, contexts in which people of different backgrounds have come together and engaged with one another (sometimes successfully, sometimes not) in the pursuit of what are often assumed to be common goals. Others are contexts better characterized by a *lack* of the kind of engagement that people would like to see—that is, contexts in which powerful outsiders impose more than they engage, and extract more than they give back (Ferguson 2006 and Sawyer 2004, for example). There is no question, however, about what all of these contexts have in common with one another, and with Ankarana: they are places in which some kind of "global connections" (Tsing 2005) continue to be made, and as such they all call on us to put aside certain assumptions we might have about "local" people living out of the "global" loop.

There is no doubt that the patterns that emerge as we zoom out from northern Madagascar help us to better situate Ankarana in the world today; sometimes, these patterns even reveal bigger pictures that we just can't see up close. The more we zoom out, however, the more we lose sight of what is so distinctive about Ankarana. This raises a good question: If what is going on in Ankarana bears such a resemblance to what is going on elsewhere in Madagascar, Africa, and the world, how special is it really? My answer to this question is what you'd probably get from most anthropologists. Whatever general points we might be heading toward in undertaking and discussing our research, the specific features of the particular cases that we rely on to get us there *always* matter. Anthropological research is not simply a matter of cataloguing the specificity of the particular lives, places, and processes revealed through conversations like those I have had with people I have met in Ankarana over the years. Like others in the field, I am also interested in what all of this specificity might teach us about the fundamental social, cultural, political, environmental, economic, and other processes that shape all human lives. What is so special about Ankarana to me for the purposes of this book, then, is that it has been the setting of the experiences, stories, and conversations recounted in these pages, and it is thus the basis of the comparisons and insights that will render distinctive the bigger picture I intend to present through them. Dadilahy was right: the specifics I found in Ankarana could not have been found anywhere else; the bigger picture they enable me to present in this book has no other primary source.

The next two chapters deal with topics that might have been studied anywhere; people everywhere work, risk, dare, buy, sell, give, take, wonder, move, scheme, and speculate in the ways that people with whom I have been working in Ankarana do. What is distinctive about what is going on in Ankarana, however, is the way in which these fundamental processes of social life have become knotted up around the nodes of global connection being made in this place. And I use the image of a knot intentionally here. As I experienced them, the settings and situations described in the following chapters have always suggested the tangled complexities of knots more than the orderly patterns of webs, networks, grids or chains that are often said to characterize our interconnected world. And given that a knot's distinctive shape comes not from the individual strands that constitute it, but from how these strands have become intertwined, trying to figure one out is more than just a matter of standing back and pulling from one direction or another. If you want to make sense of a knot, it is better to look deep into it and try to follow the convolutions that have made it the puzzle it appears to be. With this strategy in mind, the next chapter zooms back in on Ankarana, or, more precisely, on a highway-side town in the hilly terrain to the east of Ankarana National Park. No part of "the place of the rocks" has appeared more knot-like to me than the sapphire-mining and -trading centre of Ambondromifehy.

LIVING IN THE WAKE OF SAPPHIRES

By 1999, just about anyone living in Ambondromifehy who wasn't mining sapphires was likely to be trading them, and anyone who wasn't either mining or trading them was likely to be selling things to those who were; even young children took an interest, scavenging for dropped stones beneath the trading booths that lined both sides of the highway cutting through the centre of town. Sapphires had already brought thousands of migrants to this place, and they were drawing hundreds more each week. And yet sapphires were things for which people in Ambondromifehy had no use whatsoever; the only thing to do with these stones was to sell them. If it weren't for foreign buyers, in other words, the sapphires mined and traded here would be worthless. Nothing illustrated this simple fact better than the story, often told around town, of how the only ones in the region who valued these stones *before* the arrival of foreign buyers were local children who used them as ammunition in their slingshots.

The situation described here is not unusual. Millions of people around the world work to produce or procure commodities that are bound for distant, and often unknown, markets and consumers. Ambondromifehy's sapphire miners and traders thus have a great deal in common with, for example, Kenyan greenhouse workers (Dolan 2007), Papua New Guinean coffee growers (West 2012) and Guatemalan broccoli farmers (Fischer and Benson 2006), all of whom might be thought of as living in the wake of the commodities they send into the wider world; all of them watch, and sometimes wonder, as the fruits (or flowers, or beans, or vegetables, or stones) of their labour flow away from them along well-established routes of international trade that they themselves will most likely never navigate. Living in the wakes of commodities means living with the traces and impressions that these things leave behind—wages earned and spent, prices negotiated and paid, deals made and broken, pesticides sprayed and inhaled, pits dug and abandoned, rumors heard and passed along. In Ambondromifehy specifically, living in the wake of sapphires also means, as people in town often say, being "left behind" in another way—that is, by a global economy that seems to take so much away from Madagascar while offering so little benefit to Malagasy people in return.

One of the general points I hope to illustrate in this chapter is that different commodities leave distinctive traces and impressions in their wake. Obviously, sapphires aren't much like flowers, coffee beans or broccoli, nor are they as much like gold, amethyst or other commodities mined in Madagascar as you might imagine. Sapphires are, in fact, distinctive in ways that matter a great deal to the people discussed in the following sections—they are small enough to hide in your mouth, portable enough to carry around all day in search of a buyer, durable enough to be kept for months in anticipation of a foreign buyer's promised return, and individually distinctive enough to defy efforts at standardizing prices. The work involved in the mining and trading of these little stones is distinctive too, requiring that miners risk and dare in pits and caves, that traders deliberate carefully over dealings that can profit or ruin them, and that all manage the fundamental uncertainty of a trade that ultimately depends on distant, and largely unknowable, markets. To complicate matters further, many of the sapphires traded in Ambondromifehy come originally from within the boundaries of Ankarana National Park—a conservation area in which no mining or other extractive work is meant to take place.

In the next three sections, I try to impose a little order on what first struck me as a chaotic place, focusing my discussion of Ankarana's sapphire trade on three pairs of terms that capture some of the complexities and ambiguities of life and work in Ambondromifehy. First I discuss the *risking* and *daring* that were apparent in the work and consumption habits of this town's mostly young and male miners; second, I discuss the *buying* and *selling* through which the town's traders put knowledge gained through experience of the local trade to the test; and third, I discuss the difficulties that people living in the town encountered in navigating social and business networks in which what seemed like reciprocal or *gifting* relationships had the potential to be revealed as more nefarious *grifting* ones. To conclude the chapter, I narrow my focus to a final pursuit that occupied people in Ambondromifehy—the *speculating* they did regarding the future uses of the stones they mined and traded—arguing that the search for information behind these speculations may offer the greatest insights of all into the position of people living in the wake of sapphires.

Risking and Daring

Of all the words that people in Ambondromifehy used to describe their motivations for joining Ankarana's sapphire rush in the late 1990s, none better captured the uncertainties of the place than the verb *mirisky*—"to risk." To those who used this term, risking was a matter of knowingly investing time and effort in something that might not pay off in the end; it was taking a chance, hoping for a positive outcome that was far from certain.

For Koko, a 21-year-old man I met in 1999, risking began at the moment of his arrival in Ambondromifehy when, with no contacts, he had to search out the accommodations, information, and connections needed to get him started. Like so many new arrivals I met that year, Koko had come from elsewhere (in his case, a region 200 kilometres to the south) with nothing but a willingness to risk life in a place in which, it was often said, people had "met when grown"—that is, a town in which people came to live and work alongside others with whom they shared little or no background. For Koko, living in Ambondromifehy meant living far from his own "ancestral land" and the familiar social and kinship networks on which he would have relied to make his living by farming there. Not that he had to go long without family in Ambondromifehy, however. On the day he arrived, he met the man who would become his adopted "older brother" and mentor in the local trade: Jao, a 30-year-old who had been living here for two years already. Unlike Koko, Jao had come to Ambondromifehy with mining experience. Sapphire mining was different than the gold mining Jao had done before, however, so for him, too, moving here was a risk that required adapting to a range of distinctive uncertainties.

Pioneering prospectors like Jao weren't sure what they were looking for at the start. And so they worked alongside others in the same boat, using simple technology (shovels, mining bars, and flashlights or candles) to dig pits and scour cave-walls in search of sapphires. They began in areas surrounding the few small mechanical mining operations that had recently been established in the region, and then, as more people came, used what experience they had gained from this work to move on to new sites. Many of them ended up working in the forests and caves of Ankarana National Park.

A mining site inside Ankarana National Park in 2008.

A day's work at any of the mining sites around Ambondromifehy ended with miners bringing the sacks of clayey dirt collected in pits and caves to sometimes distant water sources where they could be sieved and panned through. Some miners did this key task for themselves; others left it to people (often women) they trusted. During the time I spent with him, Jao entrusted the work of sieving and panning sapphires to his "spouse" Soa, a woman he had met and moved in with just a few months before I had arrived. As I sat with Jao on a shaded riverbank while Soa worked through handfuls of the dirt he had brought out of the cave or pit inside the "taboo forest" in which he had been working most recently, the risking inherent in a life of sapphire mining was never more apparent: Soa might find something of value, or she might not.

For miners like Jao and Koko, making a living from mining required more than just a willingness to risk. To succeed, they also needed "to dare" (*mahasaky*); that is, to act boldly and with little regard for potential consequences. In mining, acts of daring included descending into unstable pits, jumping chasms in caves, defying police intent on keeping them out of Ankarana National Park, and transgressing local or inherited taboos. Where risking was always premised on a certain amount of foresight, daring suggested decisions undertaken by people working and living "for the moment" (Day, Papataxiarchis, and Stewart 1999).

MADE IN MADAGASCAR

In contrasting "risking" and "daring" here, I do not mean to imply that these terms were, or ought to be, conceived of as opposites or that miners were constantly faced with situations in which they had to choose either to risk or to dare. Rather, I have chosen to highlight these terms because they capture something of the different ways in which miners like Jao and Koko found themselves positioned, or positioned themselves, amidst the uncertainties of life in the local sapphire trade. Coming to Ambondromifehy was risky no matter what; in addition to the uncertainties of the work that would engage them here, this was a place in which neither Jao nor Koko had family, land, or other resources that might have helped them get a start. Mining also required daring, however. Consider Jao's description of a mining expedition that he and Koko undertook into the depths of the Ankarana massif. "We were supposed to leave in the night," Jao began,

> ... but we left early in the morning. We had heard that the *gendarmes* [national police] were arresting people ... but we went anyway ... when we got inside the entrance to the cave, there was lots of talking. We "dosed up" [*midozy*] ... those who smoke pot, smoked. Those who drink, drank ... then we said let's go ... we crawled for 300 or 400 metres ... that's where I got all of these cuts on my arms and knees ... and kept going and came to a chasm called the "fall of death" ... this is what we Malagasy call "goodbye father" because there is only a small rope to help you across it and if you don't know how to do it you'll fall and be killed [...] there have already been three who have fallen in the chasm and been killed here [...] then we descended 30 metres and arrived at the entrance to the cave [where we were intending to dig]. We called in to the person we knew there, and he let us in ... they don't want many people in there because it gets very hot. You can't breathe in there. We worked ... from 9 [AM] until 3 [PM] and decided to keep working until 9 at night. We crawled out through shit and piss ... the people who didn't get into the cave [and upset that they didn't] shit and pissed in the passage we returned through.

Obviously, Jao and Koko undertook this mining expedition in the context of risking—indeed, when leaving on such expeditions, they described themselves as "going to risk" rather than "to work." In the process of risking, however, they dared as well. They dared to defy the police by entering the "taboo forest," they dared to crawl along cramped passages, they dared to squeeze out rivals on their way to desired destinations, and they dared to work long hours under dangerous conditions. And their rivals dared too, showing their displeasure at being excluded in ways that their neighbours, elders, and ancestors back home would have considered transgressive and reprehensible, defiling others with their own shit and piss.

The daring evident in Jao's account of this mining trip was of a sort that is commonly attributed to young men throughout Madagascar (see, for example, Bloch 1999). In other communities in Ankarana, for example, young men who "dare to do things" were granted considerable status by both peers and elders. In traditional fighting, or *morengy*, matches especially, boys and young men put on great displays of budding machismo, strutting around a ring circled by spectators and potential challengers, their outstretched knuckle-pointed arms swinging back and forth in search of an adversary. Those who declined others' challenges to a fight were said to "not dare," while a champion was often spoken of as someone "nobody dares to take on." Significantly, though, such daring was meant to stay in the *morengy* ring. When fighters returned to their home villages, they were meant to fall in line with, rather than dare defy, the well-established orders overseen by their elders, and when they failed to do so, they were likely to be called on to answer for their behaviour by community elders or "parents" to whom they were ultimately responsible. Obviously, in the midst of the sapphire rush, Ambondromifehy was not a place in which daring young men could be brought under control so easily. In fact, there were times when living in the town felt like living in an extended and boundless *morengy* match. The problem with Ambondromifehy, I was told by Zama (the long-time resident elder introduced in the previous chapter), was not that it was a place in which people had "met when grown," but that it had become a place "without parents."

Outside of Ankarana's pits and caves, the daring of Ambondromifehy's predominantly young and male miners was especially evident in the extravagant ways in which many of them spent what they referred to as the "hot money" they earned from selling the sapphires they mined. I first heard the expression *vola mafana*, or "hot money," one afternoon in 1999 while drinking beer in the tiny hut that Jao, Koko, and Soa shared. Curious about the earnings that sapphires could provide, I had asked how much money miners in Ambondromifehy might make in a single day of work. Jao, seated on the edge of the hut's one sagging bed, answered first. His minimum daily take from the sale of the sapphires he mined, he drunkenly boasted, was 250,000 Malagasy Francs (fmg)—about $40 (Canadian) or what a sugarcane cutter might have earned for a month's work at a nearby plantation.

Jao then chinned toward Koko, hunched by the doorway rolling a joint, indicating that he had recently sold a day's worth of stones for a staggering 2.5 million fmg ($400)—enough money to hire someone to build ten simple thatched structures like the one that the four of us were crowded into. I couldn't resist asking Koko why he hadn't invested some of this windfall in a place of his own. "This is hot money," Jao answered for him, "you can't hold on to it." Koko was in no state to disagree. Instead he pulled what many Malagasy people consider to be a day's wage from his pocket and sent a neighbourhood child out for more cold beer.

The question I asked Koko about the house he hadn't built was inspired by discussions I had had in previous years with other young Malagasy men in the region for whom house building was a matter of utmost importance. Elsewhere in Ankarana, as in other parts of the island, building a house of one's own is one of the most important investments one can make, an investment not just of money (for some invest no more than their own labour) but of one's intentions for a future in a particular place and among a particular group of people (see, for example, Thomas 1998). In ideal terms, house building (along with clearing fields, buying cattle and marriage goods, getting married, supporting children, making sacrifices when necessary, etc.) is a way for young men to invest in the reproduction of the enduring social and moral orders under which they might prosper. Put another way, house building is often among the manifestations of the Malagasy "ethos of growth" (Keller 2008) introduced in the last chapter.

Obviously, Ambondromifehy was not a place conducive to this sort of investment or growth. None of the new arrivals I spoke with during the early years of the rush had any intention of staying long, meaning that few saw the point of either building substantial houses here or requesting land on which to grow rice. When men like Jao and Koko did invest in property, it was in things of the easily transportable sort—mattresses, bicycles, gold jewellery, clothes, portable stereos, etc.—that they could take with them when (not *if*) they decided to leave. Others channelled money home to family in the regions from which they had come, but for those without access to trustworthy paths of remittance, such a strategy was untenable; cautionary stories were often told of remittances that had been "eaten" (i.e., spent) by untrustworthy carriers before they ever made it to their intended destinations. Accumulating or saving money locally was not an option for most, either. Unwilling to take cash with them on mining trips for fear of having it stolen by gangs or confiscated by the police, miners had to choose between leaving it behind in Ambondromifehy (with housemates who couldn't always be trusted) or travelling 50 kilometres to deposit it in the nearest bank (requiring them to make a return trip whenever they needed cash).

So what, then, did miners like Jao and Koko do with the money they were earning from the sapphires they were selling? As the anecdote offered above suggests, they spent a great deal of it. In the days and weeks after my conversation with Jao, I asked around about "hot money" and, in response, heard dozens of stories of what struck me as outrageous behaviour—stories of miners buying rounds of drinks for dozens of hangers-on, of miners "washing the table" at which they were intending to drink by breaking and spilling a bottle of cold beer over it before sitting down, of miners hiring private cars at exorbitant rates to take them and their friends to the nightclubs of Antsiranana (100 kilometres away) for a night of partying, and of miners paying "no matter what" for sex with a particular woman in town. This was *la vie!*, I often heard, "the life!" that sapphires had brought to Ambondromifehy.

Veblen famously argued that "conspicuous consumption" of the sort I was witnessing in Ambondromifehy might be understood as a "means to reputability" (1993: 43)—that is, a means by which individuals establish and increase their reputations in the eyes of "friends and competitors" by spending lavishly on "valuable presents and expensive feasts and entertainments." There was definitely something of this going on in Ambondromifehy, with miners' "friends and competitors" (including visiting anthropologists) frequently being drawn into their efforts at establishing reputations as successful, charismatic, and daring young men. Freely giving and spending money was also obviously important, however, to the creation and fostering of the social and work networks that miners relied on in the midst of a profoundly uncertain trade. In fact, Jao and Koko's brotherhood developed not through acts of common investment in the kind of enduring projects that kin might share elsewhere in Madagascar (through clearing land, digging wells, or maintaining sacred sites together, for example), but through more ephemeral acts of common consumption (drinking, smoking pot, and gambling together) that were better suited to the circumstances of the place. Focusing simply on what spending "hot money" did for those who engaged in it only tells part of the story, however. To make sense of the consumption habits of young men like Jao and Koko, we must also consider all the things that Ambondromifehy's conspicuous consumers were *not* spending money on in this context.

I wasn't the only one surprised by stories of "hot money." Zama and other long-time residents of Ambondromifehy were taken aback too, though they were inclined to see the consumption going on around them more as wasteful than as an interesting sociological phenomenon. They criticized young men like Jao and Koko for "eating" or "killing" the money they had earned, destroying its potential by spending in ways that indicated a lack of foresight. With such objections in mind, we might do better to think of these young men as "daring," rather than "conspicuous," consumers—that is, as young men whose consumption habits reflected a way of being that is commonly attributed to young men in Madagascar. Spending money on *la vie* meant *not* investing it in ways that might mark their passage to the responsible status that elders like Zama expected them to be assuming. By not building houses, buying cattle or fixing up the tombs of their ancestors in the sometimes distant "ancestral lands" from which they had migrated, they daringly defied the obligations inherent in lives they might have been living as farmers and herders elsewhere on the island. By similarly not digging wells, planting fields or helping to care for elders and sacred sites in and around Ambondromifehy, meanwhile, they avoided investing in ways that might have rooted them locally and under the authority of nearby elders like Zama. For distant parents who sent requests for support from home regions, the main obstacle to reigning in their daring descendants was distance itself; for local elders like Zama, meanwhile, the problem was that Ambondromifehy had come to be a place "without parents" at all—that is, a place overwhelmed by young people who had little cause to listen to elders like him.

Although Jao and Koko clearly took a great deal of pleasure in *la vie* that sapphire earnings enabled them to live, we must be careful not to romanticize these rebellious young consumers. As daring as it might have been in the moment, Jao's habit of spending all of the "hot money" in his pocket inevitably precipitated the sobering need to go out and risk again. Indeed, Jao's attitude toward both "the life!" and his own life was markedly different from one day to the next—from occasions when money was plentiful to those when it was desperately needed. On mornings after nights of extravagant spending he bemoaned his situation, sometimes even accusing Soa and Koko of stealing from him. One morning, showing me the scars that crawling through pits and passages had left on his back and belly, he told me that he "kills himself" when he mines. And yet his risking, daring, and daring consumption continued. When I ran into him on a return visit to Ambondromifehy a year after our first meeting, he assured me that all was as I had remembered it. Although he no longer shared a house with Koko or a bed with Soa, he continued to live "the life." Years later, I learned that he had moved on to risking in another mining rush in southern Madagascar where, rumour had it, he remained as daring as ever.

For many of Ambondromifehy's residents, sapphire mining was only the start. Consider the case of Abdou, a 21-year-old man I interviewed immediately after he had sold a single sapphire he had mined for 800,000 fmg (about $120). When I asked him what he was going to do with this money, he replied:

> I'm going to buy sapphires and turn them around ... I'll sell them, put my money to work, and make even more than I have now. [What about *la vie*? I asked] ... I am not going to do *la vie*, I won't drink alcohol, I'm not going to sleep with any women ... If I spend all my money on women, when it's done, they won't concern themselves with me! ... In the past I didn't know. I didn't think much. I bought clothes and shoes ... and the women! All of the women, all of the prostitutes did well from me. Now I think. I remember. I am no longer a child but an adult. I've got a beard ... I've got children. I've got a wife here. I'm going to buy and sell.

According to Abdou, the move from daring consumption to risky investment required that he grow up. As a man ages, he implied, he should give up the daring practices and strategies of youth in favour of the deliberative ones of men old enough to have beards and children. Abdou assured me that there was nothing inherently "hot" about the money one earns from sapphires; the heat of "hot money," he contended, was generated by the imaginations of young men like Jao and Koko. And as noted in the previous section, he was not the only one in town to think so. Elders like Zama thought so too, as did most of the women I interviewed in Ambondromifehy.

Although it was mostly men who mined sapphires in Ambondromifehy, women played an important role in the town and the local sapphire trade as well. Some women arrived during the height of the rush with the intention of trying their own hands at mining, but most I interviewed claimed not to be up to the kind of daring required of this work, and so they made do through arrangements in which they worked, and often lived, with miners as Soa had: sieving and panning their dirt, and sometimes even selling their stones to traders. Other women had come with the intention of earning their living from sapphire miners rather than from sapphires themselves: selling the food, beer, and sex that the town's daring consumers were willing to pay so dearly for. The most successful women in town, however, were those who found a place in the sapphire trade itself. By 1999, at least one-quarter of the town's sapphire traders were women.

When I returned to Ambondromifehy in 2003 with the intention of focusing specifically on how the local sapphire trade actually worked, I was especially curious to know whether the stereotypically masculine habits favoured by so many of the town's miners had a place in the complex business of buying and selling sapphires. To spark conversation, I asked around about whether men or women made better traders. As I might have predicted, some men answered that since only men "dare [to pay high] prices" for big and potentially valuable individual stones, they are the most likely to earn big windfalls from their transactions. Women who dealt in large quantities of lower-cost stones, meanwhile, saw their strategy as the more sensible one. Roby, a 28-year-old trader, repeated a common refrain, noting that women dare less but "calculate/reflect more [than men do]," by which she meant that women in the trade are more concerned with the possibility of steady earnings than with big scores. This is so, she continued, " because men have made them suffer." Women, Roby suggested, were more motivated to save and invest their money carefully out of a desire to free themselves from having to rely on others (men in particular). The future that Roby imagined for herself—in a "foreign-style house," complete with a pool, in a nearby town—did *not* include a husband.

What I learned from Roby and other traders that year is that Ambondromifehy's sapphire trade was not nearly as disorganized as I had originally imagined it to be. In fact, this trade operated according to many of the principles of the Moroccan bazaar described by Geertz (1979). Like participants in any bazaar economy, traders in Ambondromifehy had to concern themselves with more than just getting their hands on what was being traded. Reliable information about the different qualities of sapphires, the state of the local market, and the demands of foreign buyers was a local trader's greatest asset, meaning that much of their time and effort was spent searching out information they lacked and protecting information they had, activities that, as Geertz suggests, are "the name of the game" in any bazaar economy (1979: 125). Good information would allow a trader like Roby to take advantage of the "knowledge differentials" (215) that enable successful players in all bazaars to profit from the relative ignorance of others. Insufficient, or wrong, information, on the other hand, could be ruinous; as Geertz notes, "the only thing that can hurt you" in a bazaar economy " is what you don't know, and someone else does" (216). Not surprisingly, then, the greatest fortunes made in Ambondromifehy's sapphire trade were made at the very start of the rush, not because this was a time when the most valuable sapphires were coming out of the region's pits and caves, but because this was when the knowledge differential between experienced sapphire buyers and novice sapphire sellers was the greatest. In the first year of the boom, foreign and Malagasy traders were buying up the region's sapphires at shockingly low prices, measuring what they were buying not by the carat or gram, but by the *kapohaka*—the standard measure of a condensed-milk can (around one cup in volume) by which rice, beans, and other dry goods are sold in food markets throughout Madagascar. Sellers simply didn't know how much they were losing out in the process. Over time, though, as more foreign buyers arrived, and local traders discovered through experience more of the information they were lacking, circumstances came to favour the careful, deliberative strategies of women like Roby.

Most sapphires traded along the strip in 2003 were bought and sold by weight, in groupings of anywhere from two to upwards of a thousand; only sapphires of unusually large size, or high quality, were traded individually. In most cases, buyers and sellers knew one another quite well, which meant that their encounters were, as Geertz might put it, "confrontation[s] between intimate antagonists" (1979: 225), of the sort one finds in all bazaars. Sellers would come to one of the town's hundreds of trading booths asking anywhere from two to five times what they were willing to accept for what they were selling, and buyers were likely to counter with an offer of one-half to one-fifth of what they were willing to pay. From there, bargaining would either falter quickly or proceed slowly until one or the other, usually the seller in cases I observed, gave in, agreeing to a price somewhere in the middle of the two initial quotes.

The terms that buyers used to evaluate the sapphires they were scrutinizing indicated both foreign influence and local creativity. The region's sapphires ran the spectrum from *jaune-jaune* (yellowish) through *eau-vive* (the light blue colour of a Malagasy brand of bottled water) to *bleu royale* (the "royal blue" valued by English-speaking jewellery customers); in terms of size, they came as small as a *loambary* (a fraction the size of a grain of rice) and as large as a *grosseur* (large stones of up to 10 grams). Also important, and harder to discern, were the internal properties of stones—whether they were transparent (*transparent*), milky (*misy ronono*, or "has milk") or opaque (*hopaka*), for example, and whether or not they had imperfections such as inclusions or cracks, or desirable features such as the distinctive makings of a star-sapphire. It was not just the existence of all of these variables and terms that made the local trade so complicated, however; it was

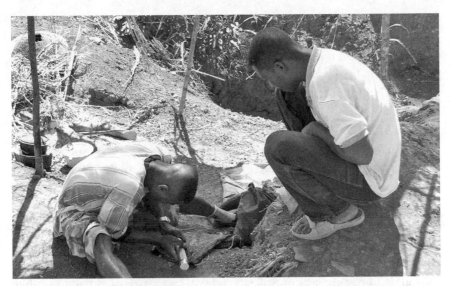
A mobile trader scrutinizes sapphires at a mining site.

the fact that none of these variables existed in isolation in any single stone. Buying and selling sapphires was so complicated because each sapphire was unique and had to be evaluated as such. And so Roby and other traders spent hours seated in their roadside booths, scales and calculators close at hand, peering deep into one after another sapphire rolled around between thumb and forefinger. Scrutinizing sapphires in this way was never simply a matter of stalling or holding out for a better price. It was a calculating task through which a buyer's knowledge of the trade was put to the test.

During a trading day's inevitable slumps, Roby could be found in a different pose: hovering over a pile of sapphires, picking up, examining, and then moving individual stones to several smaller piles to the side. This was *triage*, the means by which buyers sorted through and divvied up previous purchases in ways that put their knowledge of the advantages and disadvantages of the many distinct qualities of sapphires (and combinations thereof) to use. A hypothetical example should help illustrate how *triage* worked. Say Roby had spent one million fmg by buying a total of one kilogram of small sapphires from a variety of sellers at an average price of 1000 fmg/gram. Through careful *triage*, she might move 50 grams (1/20th of the total) to a separate pile that could sell, to the right buyer, for 5000 fmg/gram, five times the original price paid. Provided that the remaining 950 grams in her stock could be sold for no less than what she had paid for it, then she would earn a tidy profit from nothing more than careful sorting in light of good knowledge.

For one of Ambondromifehy's stationary buyers, a dream seller was a young miner fresh out of his pit on market day—someone who had come to town, dirt still on his pants, with the intention of selling his sapphires and filling up on distractions and supplies before heading back to his work. Miners who unloaded their stones in this way did just what the buyers to whom they sold would eventually have to do themselves: they transferred the risk of holding something with no local use value, but great potential exchange value, onto someone else. And for miners especially, such transactions took place not only amidst the ambiguities of an uncertain market, but in the face of the realities of daily life—food costs money, and, as I was often reminded, "you can't eat sapphires." Miners were also quick to sell their stones because they generally knew the least about the current state of the trade and were therefore always in a poor position to judge whether the first price offered for the stones they were looking to sell would ever be bettered. They were certainly not faced with the luxury of an auction-like situation, in which potential buyers competed with one another in a process most beneficial to sellers. The only thing that a miner could be sure of was that a price offered for what they had to sell would stand only momentarily. A buyer would *never* offer the same price later in the day, knowing that the sapphires under consideration had already been scrutinized by others around town; after all, buyers had no interest in being the highest bidder in the very market into which they most likely intended to resell.

In the end, all of the sapphires circulating in Ambondromifehy were destined to be sold to foreign buyers, mostly Thai and West African men based in the city of Antsiranana, who would take them out of the country and on to the distant centres of the international sapphire trade, where they would be transformed into the cut and polished gemstones that foreign consumers know best. (I discuss this further in Chapter 4.) On return trips to Ambondromifehy, foreign buyers brought merchandise with them—the scales and specialty flashlights that traders needed to scrutinize sapphires, as well as the watches and portable electronics found in market stalls all over town—and with the sale of these products they subsidized their next round of buying. As long as there were sapphires to be found in Ankarana, there would always be sapphires to buy in Ambondromifehy. As was made clear above, sapphires can't be eaten, like locally grown rice, or transformed into products for sale to local consumers, like locally mined gold or locally produced lumber. The only thing to do with sapphires was to sell them, and the only local buyers of these stones were people, whether Malagasy or foreign, who intended to sell them again for profit. This was the "secret" that foreign buyers knew about Ambondromifehy's sapphire trade, I was once told, and this is why such foreigners would always do best in the end.

Toward the end of my stay in 2003, I travelled to Antsiranana to visit Omar, one of the foreign buyers I had met in Ambondromifehy. He laughed at the term *Africain* with which he and others were often labelled by Malagasy people, reminding me, as he often reminded the local traders with whom he dealt, that Madagascar is part of Africa too. In fact, Omar had been born in Sierra Leone and had grown up around the work that had brought him to Madagascar, learning the business of gemstone trading while working alongside his father in mining towns in Guinea, Nigeria, Zambia, and Angola. As you might imagine, such experience gave Omar a distinctive perspective on Ambondromifehy's trade. Ankarana's sapphires, he told me, were not of very good quality; in fact, the region's stones were all destined for Thailand, he claimed, where they would they would have to undergo a particular kind of value-adding treatment that wasn't being used anywhere else in the world (a point to which I will return in Chapter 4)—a "secret" treatment, he specified, of which even he didn't know the details. Not that it mattered. For Omar, as for the Malagasy traders who supplied him, all that mattered was that his connections in Thailand would buy what he had to sell, and that he would come out ahead in the end. And this, he told me, was never a sure thing. He claimed that he and other foreign traders were not impervious to the risks that Malagasy traders faced. Indeed, like Roby and other traders in Ambondromifehy, he sought information as much as he sought sapphires themselves, speaking by phone with contacts in the Thai trade on a daily basis, for example, and regularly checking on international currency exchange rates posted at the bank down the street. Indeed, a day spent with Omar confirmed what traders in Ambondromifehy assumed. The international sapphire trade was no less a bazaar than the one that had taken shape in Ankarana—it was a complex and uncertain trade character-ized by profound "knowledge differentials" among differently positioned players intending to profit from their dealings with one another.

Gifting and Grifting

Based on the previous two sections, some might be tempted to conclude that what made Ambondromifehy so different from other communities in Ankarana was a product of the particular kinds of market exchange that figured so prominently in people's lives there—exchanges of "hot money" for rounds of beer, for example, or of sapphires for money. Exchanges involving money were not the only ones going on in this town, however. In this section, I discuss "gifting" and "grifting," two other kinds of exchange that also contributed to Ambondromifehy's distinctive boom-time development. I might have avoided confusion here by using the term "reciprocity" in place of "gifting," and either "cheating" or "conning" in place of "grifting," but for reasons that should become clear as I proceed, using terms that might be confused with each other helps make my point. For people in Ambondromifehy, the kinds of exchange with which I associate the terms "gifting" and "grifting" were themselves all too easily confused with one another, and the possibility of such confusion tells us a great deal about the uncertainties of life in this place (Walsh 2009).

The form of exchange I refer to here as "gifting" is most commonly associated with Mauss's influential essay, published in English as *The Gift* (1990), concerning the significance of giving, receiving, and reciprocating gifts in human society. Mauss's vision of reciprocity has been much debated over the years, but even a newcomer to his work will likely be familiar with the fundamental idea, as well as the power, of what he referred to as "the gift." If you have ever been offered and accepted a birthday present, a dinner invitation or a car ride from someone else and have then felt obliged to reciprocate by eventually offering something like it in return, you know very well the social force of gifting. Gifting has the power to embroil people in social relationships that move to a certain rhythm—give, receive, reciprocate, give, receive, reciprocate, give, receive, reciprocate, and so on. Unlike the staccato rhythm of market exchange, in which impersonal individual transactions tend to have clear beginnings and endings, the rhythm of gifting is ideally continuous and likely to become more pronounced and dependable the longer it goes on.

Many of the relationships that took root in Ambondromifehy during the early years of the sapphire rush were established with, and propagated through, exchanges that were meant, ideally, to follow the rhythm of gifting. Zama and other long-time residents of the community gave new arrivals permission to settle and provided them access to the tree at which they might seek blessing; Jao gave his "brother" Koko—a relative stranger—access to his own mining pit, lessons on mining, and a place to sleep on the floor of his house; Koko gave hangers-on more cold beer than they could drink; male miners gave sacks of freshly mined dirt to women who asked. Such generous acts were generally spoken of as manifestations of Malagasy *fomba* or "custom"—that is, as acts of a sort that Malagasy people living in any community ought to do for one another and for the betterment of all, and thus acts that could not be answered with payments of money. Although the relationships that came out of such gifting in Ambondromifehy sometimes brought benefits to givers, the promise of such benefits was never spoken of as a motivation. If anything, what motivated gifting in Ambondromifehy was confidence—in particular, givers' confidence that recipients of their hospitality, support, sacks of dirt, and trust were operating with a similar mindset and would, therefore, return the favour if and when called upon to do so.

Gifting often worked just as advocates of Malagasy custom might have hoped. For example, several recipients of Zama's ancestors' blessing did eventually return to the sacred tree outside of Zama's house with promised offerings; Koko took Jao's side in fights over access to a pit they shared; recipients of Koko's largesse wound up buying rounds of drinks of their own; and women who found sapphires in the sacks of dirt they had been given shared their earnings with miners. In other cases, however, givers' confidence in recipients was revealed to have been *mis*placed, and givers lamented accordingly. Zama accused newcomers who failed to live up to the obligations that came with the blessings they received at the base of his tree of having "burned" his community, for example, and Jao eventually ended his brotherhood with Koko by accusing him of stealing sapphires that they were meant to share. Even the ideally reciprocal, mutually beneficial, relationships that developed between women and men in Ambondromifehy risked revealing themselves as something other than what they seemed. In the early years of the rush, stories circulated about the dangers of "red suitcase" women who were rumoured to lull miners into comfortable, reciprocal, and mutually beneficial relationships over a matter of months, only to eventually leave them without notice, taking all of their accumulated earnings and possessions with them upon departure. Meanwhile, stories were told of men who had headed off to new mining booms elsewhere in Madagascar, leaving women behind with nothing but unfulfilled promises of an eventual return.

Rumours and experiences of misplaced confidence reminded those who spoke of them of the ambiguous and dangerous side of engaging in gifting in Ambondromifehy. As useful as reciprocity could be in a place in which people had "met when grown," recipients could never be counted on to reciprocate in expected ways. Even relationships that seemed to have been well founded in repeated acts of giving, receiving, and reciprocating risked being revealed as something else: what we might call "grifting" relationships.

According to Maurer (1974), who studied the practices of American con artists (or "grifters") of the 1920s and 1930s, grifting is not the same as stealing. Unlike thieves, grifters do not *take* what they want from others, but, rather, convince others to *give* them what they want by preying on their confidence, often lulling them into what seem to be mutually beneficial, reciprocal relationships based on familiar patterns of exchange. When grifting works, in other words, it takes victims by surprise. Where the aforementioned rhythm of gifting is ideally regular and continuous—give, receive, reciprocate; give, receive, reciprocate; give, receive, reciprocate; etc.—the rhythm of grifting differs by only one very important beat: give, receive, reciprocate; give, receive, reciprocate; give, receive ... *nothing*. Indeed, all it takes for an apparently reciprocal and mutually beneficial relationship to be revealed as something more sinister is for one or another of its participants to receive after giving and then leave. In a place inhabited by people who had "met when grown," in which *everyone* was intending to leave at some point, you might imagine why celebrations of the reciprocity encouraged by Malagasy custom in Ambondromifehy tended to be tempered by an awareness of the ever-present possibility of sudden departures.

Concerns over the possibility of being deceived by what appeared to be well-mannered "visitors," hard-working "brothers," and supportive "spouses" mirrored people's concerns over the many possibilities for deception opened up by the work that had brought all of them together. Subtle forms of deception figured centrally in all bargaining over sapphires in Ambondromifehy—indeed, here, as in any bazaar economy, traders had to concern themselves not only with "whom, what, and how much to believe" (Geertz 1979: 203), but also with whom, about what, and how much to *deceive*. Sellers lied to buyers about the prices they were looking for, and buyers lied to sellers about what they were willing to pay; it was only as bargaining advanced that prices volleyed back and forth got closer to what each could live with. Where pre-existing relationships between buyers and sellers existed, one would often lie to the other about losing money on a previous transaction in pursuit of a more advantageous price. Of course, those to whom they were lying had heard, and might have told, such lies before. Buyers inevitably lied about the state of the market for stones being offered them, and sellers lied about how much they had paid for stones that they were looking to resell. Knowledgeable traders would sometimes do their less knowledgeable bargaining antagonists a double disservice by haggling for a lower price while, at the same time, lecturing them with lies about all that was wrong with their stones. Maybe the craftiest sort of deception, however, came at the end of a bargaining session. Neither buyer nor seller would even hint at being pleased with a transaction, though they often were of course; each wanted to leave the other with the impression of having been given, rather than having given up, a good deal so that they might better position themselves as being owed something in future transactions.

However deceptive they might seem, and however much they preyed on the misplaced confidence of those who lost out in them, trading practices like the ones discussed here were widely recognized as part of the *biznesy* of trading in sapphires. Other common practices were not so acceptable. A trader described one such ruse:

> You go to sell [a sapphire] to a Thai buyer, but they don't like it ... you hide the fact that they didn't like it and give it to a miner who has just come out of the bush, in dirty clothes. Even if they aren't out of the bush, [this miner] can put on old clothes and cover themselves with mud ... and put dirt on the sapphire. Then [this miner] makes as though he is coming from [the bush] and is called to by buyers [from their booths] ... [the miner] shows them the sapphire and tells them that no one else has seen it ... that it is a secret sapphire ... if you [i.e., the buyer] saw it, you'd buy it quickly before anyone else gets to see it. ... it depends on how well you know stones. If you are slow, if you don't know stones, you can be burned by this. Often people are burned by stones that are said to be new, but that have already been around.

In a way that nicely illustrates the great complexity of trading in Ambondromifehy's sapphire bazaar, victims of this ploy were burned by presuming a knowledge differential that they expected would allow them to take advantage of someone else.

Of all the deceptions going on in Ambondromifehy, none was more widely reviled than the practice of buying stones on credit, taking them away, and then never paying for them. And all agreed that the most egregious practitioners of this offence were foreign traders. How could Malagasy traders fall victim to such a simple con? The following case should help illustrate just how easily an apparently beneficial gifting relationship can be revealed as a potentially ruinous grifting one.

Madame Fernand was one of Ambondromifehy's most successful Malagasy traders. She arrived early on in the rush, using money inherited from her late French husband to buy up large quantities of sapphires at low prices.

After selling these stones to foreign buyers, she invested her profits widely around town, establishing a large nightclub on the trading strip, developing and running a fleet of bush-taxis, and, of course, trading sapphires. Madame Fernand referred to and joked with the miners and other traders from whom she bought stones in ways that signalled reciprocal and caring relationships, calling them "brother" and "sister," for example. She gave money to those who requested help, insisting to me that these were *cadeaux* or "gifts" and not loans. She kept a bottle of fresh water at the ready, and offered it to any thirsty passers-by who asked, assuring them, and me, that we are, after all, "one family."

When I suggested to Madame Fernand that her generosity revealed what a savvy businesswoman she was, she answered that, in fact, she expected nothing in return for what she gave. What kind of a person would refuse water to a thirsty miner?, she wondered. Certainly not someone like Madame Fernand, who spoke of the importance of Malagasy custom and the sharing, reciprocity, and mutual responsibility it encouraged. And yet it was clear that Madame Fernand depended on her relationships with the "brothers" and "sisters'" from whom she bought her sapphires for more than just conversation; given her experience and connections, she generally knew more about the state of the local trade than they did, and she was generally able to put this knowledge differential to profitable use in the dealings that would often follow glasses of water and other "gifts" offered and accepted.

It wasn't only Madame Fernand's knowledge of sapphires that had made her such a success in the local trade, however. She also benefitted greatly from the profitable relationships she had developed early on with several West African buyers based in Antsiranana. Knowing what kinds of sapphires these foreign traders were looking for, and what they would be willing to pay for such stones, was invaluable to her. Over time, as repeated dealings with these foreign buyers produced more benefits for all, her relationships with them began to take on the appearance of those founded in the reciprocity of Malagasy custom. She flirted and joked with them (in broken French, their common language) as she would have done with a spouse or brother-in-law; she offered and accepted lifts to and from the city; she ensured that they were served cold drinks and snacks whenever they came to Ambondromifehy. Most fateful of all, though, she began to accept their requests for credit, allowing them to take away her sapphires without actually paying for them. This confidence served her well for several years, as the buyers to whom she entrusted her stones always returned from Thailand, as promised, with what they owed her and with new orders to boot. It was only a matter of time, however, before Madame Fernand was burned by an African trader who left Ambondromifehy, and Madagascar, with $20,000 worth of stones that he would never end up paying for. A few years later, it happened again.

When I asked Madame Fernand why she didn't use some of the money she had made in Ambondromifehy to travel to Thailand to sell her sapphires herself, she said that she had already thought of, and dismissed, the possibility. What would she do if she ever got there?, she asked. She knew few people in the trade there, and even those she did know couldn't be trusted to work in her interests. She understood, in other words, that the hard-won skills, knowledge, and connections that had made her such an important player in the local sapphire trade were not transferable internationally. The fact is that no matter how good she got at negotiating, and profiting from, the complex relationships that enmeshed her in Ambondromifehy, Madame Fernand had been destined from the start to be among the most vulnerable players in this local sapphire trade's global counterpart. Players like Omar, the foreign buyer I discussed at the end of the previous section, would always have the advantage over someone like Madame Fernand, and not just because of the knowledge that would help him negotiate the complexities of Thailand's sapphire bazaar. Foreign buyers also had the great advantage on which most grifters ultimately rely: mobility. Indeed, whatever their professed solidarity with their Malagasy counterparts, foreign buyers, Omar included, were themselves destined to eventually leave after receiving and … never come back.

Speculating in the Wake of Sapphires

By organizing the previous three sections around the activities and concerns that occupied people in Ambondromifehy's sapphire trade, I have tried to offer a sense of some of the complexities involved in what some readers may have assumed must be a simple business—clearly, there was more going on in this place than pulling stones out of the ground and then selling them to foreigners. I have also tried to portray the complexity of work and social lives shaped by these activities and concerns. Although the town's miners and traders risked a lot by immersing themselves in the uncertainties of Ankarana's sapphire trade, it should be clear that they did so as active, and sometimes daring, players, choosing where to mine, what to buy, when to sell, whom to trust, and how much to deceive, all of their decisions based on the best of their often considerable, and hard-won, knowledge. No amount of daring or knowledge could change the simplest fact of life in the wake of sapphires, however. As Madame Fernand had learned, and as others like her often repeated, everyone in Ambondromifehy was destined to be "left behind" eventually, and there was very little they could do about it.

To conclude this chapter, I consider one last activity that sometimes occupied the people with whom I spent time in Ambondromifehy—the speculating that they did about the future uses of sapphires. Considered in light of the overview just offered, such speculating reveals the significant limits that are simultaneously imposed and revealed by living in the wake of sapphires.

As chaotic and confusing a place as Ambondromifehy could seem at times, it was also a remarkably easy place in which to do the kind of research that helped me understand it better. Where days spent in quiet farming villages elsewhere in the region tended to involve a lot of wandering around and looking for people to talk with, days in Ambondromifehy were almost always spent in continuous conversation. I would be lucky to cover 200 metres of the trading strip in a single day; leaving one trading booth, I would get drawn into another by the calls of bored traders.

In mining areas, too, people tended to congregate in ways that favoured a curious interloper like me—women grouped around water sources panning through dirt, for example, or men waiting their turns at the edges of a shared mining pit. The longer I stayed, and more I returned, the deeper my connections with the people I was speaking with became, and, before

Ambondromifehy's trading strip on a slow day.

MADE IN MADAGASCAR

long, they started to answer my questions with questions of their own: Where is Bangkok? Why do the sapphires mined in Ankarana go there? Why is it that only certain types of foreigners come here to buy sapphires? How are distant events, such as wars or global health crises, connected to fluctuations in sapphire prices? Questioners assumed that as a Malagasy-speaking foreigner who was clearly very interested in the sapphire trade, I might make a good source of information.

Of all the questions I was asked in Ambondromifehy, none surprised me more than the one I heard most often: What are sapphires used for? Many of the miners and traders I spoke with had heard that these stones were used in the production of jewellery worn by foreigners, but this possibility seemed implausible to most. When I asked my questioners what *they* thought these stones might be used for, I heard a wide range of speculations. One common suggestion was that sapphires were being used in the production of expensive electronics—in CD players, airplane and helicopter navigation equipment, and timers or clocks, for example. Another was that the durability of sapphires made them essential to the production of bulletproof vests, indestructible highways, and impenetrable walls in the houses of foreign billionaires. Yet another possibility was that sapphires were being melted down and moulded into the durable face coverings of expensive watches or the windows of spacecraft. Most commonly, though, I heard it speculated that sapphires were being used in the production of bullets and bombs. Sapphires, many supposed, made their way from northern Madagascar to Bangkok, and then on to America where they were transformed into armaments. To such speculators, news reports of American military action in Iraq and Afghanistan through the 2000s only confirmed the likelihood that Ambondromifehy's sapphires were destined, ultimately, for use in distant war zones.

I could speculate at length myself concerning the origins of these speculations. Some traders reported that they had heard these things on the radio or had seen magazine ads for products such as watches that featured the word "sapphire" in their marketing. Others had based speculations on their own understandings of the inherent material qualities of sapphires; one Malagasy trader explained, for example, that the milky interior that Thai traders often sought in Ankarana's sapphires was caused by a gas that, once extracted from these stones, was what foreigners were really after. Speculators were also likely extrapolating from what they knew of other minerals found in Madagascar, resources that might well be melted down and remoulded (gold and silver) or used in the production of watches (quartz) and armaments (uranium). With these points in mind, it is not so unreasonable that people in Ambondromifehy speculated as they did. As they saw it, the possibilities they suggested were certainly more reasonable than the idea that sapphires were being used in the production of jewellery. Sapphires are simply too expensive, too plain, too small, and too common to be used in jewellery, I was assured at various times. They are not nearly as beautiful as gold, silver, or even amethyst, all of which have a long history of use in Madagascar's own jewellery industry; and yet they sell for much, much more. Sapphires *must* have some other use.

My first inclination in trying to make sense of these questions, speculations, and doubts about sapphires was to think of them as the inevitable products of a global economy that, as we are so often told, brings together people with different cultural values. As far as I knew at the time, the sapphires coming out of Ambondromifehy were destined to be used in the manufacture of what we, following Appadurai, might call "luxuries," things such as rings, earrings, and necklaces, "whose principal use" would never be practical but, rather, "rhetorical and social" (1986: 38) within contexts far removed from this northern Malagasy mining town. A locally mined sapphire might end up as part of a one-of-a-kind anniversary gift for a one-of-a-kind spouse, maybe, and then worn to communicate subtle messages about its wearer's self to like-minded others. That the miners and traders I was talking with might have found such a fate impossible to believe shouldn't have been surprising. We might even imagine that Ambondromifehy's speculators speculated as they did because they just didn't have a *taste* for the uses to which foreigners would end up putting sapphires, much as they didn't (as you may not) have a taste for shark-fin soup, sea-cucumber stir-fry or any of the other foreign luxuries made from commodities procured originally in northern Madagascar.

We must be careful, however, of assuming too wide a divide between Ambondromifehy's miners and traders and the foreign consumers who were being served by their work. These two groups have more in common than some might assume. Roby certainly knew that jewellery can be valuable and beautiful, for example, just as Jao knew that consumption choices can communicate aspects of a consumer's self, and Madame Fernand knew that all sapphires are distinctive. Even more obviously, however, local miners and traders understood that they participated in the same global-bazaar economy as the ultimate users of sapphires, and, as Ambondromifehy's speculators saw it, what separated them from other players in such an economy was not cultural differences but knowledge differentials—that is, not what they did and didn't *value* about these little stones, but what they did and didn't (and could and couldn't) *know* about them. Therefore, their questions and speculations didn't originate in idle curiosity and oblivious ignorance but, rather, in a well-founded awareness of the harmful potential of the "*known* ignorances" (Geertz 1979: 125; italics in original) that plague all players in a bazaar economy—that is, the ignorances of those who know how little they know and, with that, know how marginal this makes them.

The answers I gave to miners and traders who asked me about the uses of sapphires were almost always met with the same disbelieving response: "impossible." The fact that I echoed untrustworthy foreign traders in reporting that locally mined sapphires *were*, in fact, primarily used in the production of jewellery indicated to my questioners either that I was as far out of the loop as they were, or, more sinisterly, that I was as committed as others to guarding the secrets of the global trade that their work supplied. Since the global sapphire trade was assumed to operate in the bazaar-like fashion of the local one, there was no question as to why foreigners involved in the trade might withhold knowledge or lie about what was becoming of Ankarana's sapphires. One trader summed up his distrust of supposedly truth-telling foreigners as follows:

> if [foreign buyers] said, "let me tell you what the use of [sapphires] is" ... I'd be looking for a way to get them [overseas] myself. Many of us Malagasy have enough money to pay our way to Bangkok, but we're afraid. We don't know ... the system for taking them there ... we don't know.

As comments like this suggest, it may be that what Ambondromifehy's speculators had come to know best of all about the global sapphire trade through their experiences in the local one was not just how little they knew, but also how being left behind in Madagascar limited any efforts they might have undertaken to make up the knowledge differentials that were bound to work against them. To many with whom I spoke, nothing illustrated the marginal position of Malagasy people in the global economy more pithily than the previously mentioned story of how sapphires had once been used as slingshot pellets. How could something so valuable on the international market have remained unknown to Malagasy people for so long?, they wondered. For that matter: What else might there be in Ankarana's forests and caves that foreigners know about and Malagasy people don't?

As noted in the Introduction, Ambondromifehy's speculators didn't need to go far to observe the kind of foreign consumers for whom local sapphires were destined. In fact, during some times of the year, several car- and minibus-loads of foreigners would zip along the town's trading strip every day on their way to the main entrance of Ankarana National Park, just 20 kilometres to the south. The fact that new facilities had been built in the nearby community of Mahamasina to welcome these visitors just before the start of the region's sapphire rush, and that the number of visiting foreigners increased steadily in the years following the rush, provided fodder for just the sort of speculation you might expect. "They are looking for something there," one trader noted,

> but I don't know what.... They're not going there [i.e., to the park] to take pictures ... I don't know whether it's the "wealth from the belly of the land" [i.e., sapphires] or mercury or something else. There is a reason.

The idea that these foreigners were, as he and others in town had been assured by local conservation officials, tourists intent on "taking nothing but pictures and leaving nothing but footprints" in Ankarana National Park was as hard to believe as the idea that the region's sapphires were being used in the manufacture of jewellery. Clearly, these foreigners were up to something. In the next chapter I consider just what that was.

THE PROMISE AND PRACTICE OF ECOTOURISM IN ANKARANA

Ankarana National Park is more than just a source of sapphires for the miners and traders discussed in the previous chapter; it is also a source of great wonderment for the thousands of foreigners who travel to the region to visit it every year. For a preliminary sense of why foreigners are drawn to this place, consider how Ankarana National Park is described in a recent edition of the *Lonely Planet Guide to Madagascar*: it is

> ... a striking and undeveloped fantasyland that's home to uniquely Madagascan sights: psychedelic forests of ruby-red *tsingy* [limestone pinnacles] sit next to semi-dry forests where nocturnal sportive lemurs pop their heads out of holes by your feet. Running through and under the *tsingy* are hidden forest-filled canyons and subterranean rivers, some containing crocodiles. There are bat filled grottos and mysterious caves steeped in legend and history, where traditional rites are still held and *fady* [taboo] is strictly observed. (Anderson et al. 2008: 186)

No wonder Ankarana National Park consistently figures among the top ecotourism destinations in Madagascar (Freudenberger 2010: 24). As of 2012, it has even made it to the number-two spot on *Lonely Planet*'s online list of "Top Picks" for visitors to the island (*Lonely Planet* 2012).

In this chapter I trace Ankarana National Park's transformation from the little-known conservation reserve it appeared to be in the late 1980s into the popular ecotourist destination that it has become. As the evocative description offered above suggests, and as I will discuss further in Chapter 4, there is no doubt that what draws ecotourists to this place are its most spectacular features—its charismatic lemurs, its caves, its "psychedelic forests," and so on. If we want to understand how the region's ecotourist trade has actually developed, however, and how it has come to involve and affect people living around the park, we need to think about more than what makes it attractive. That Ankarana National Park has become the ecotouristic "top pick" it is today also owes a great deal to the thinking and efforts that have gone into making it so accessible to foreigners over the past 20 years.

The Promise of Ecotourism in Ankarana

During my first several stays in Ankarana in the early 1990s, I rarely ran into foreign tourists. At that time, a foreigner had to be either very adventurous or very rich to even attempt a visit to what was then still called the Ankarana Special Reserve; the permits needed to enter the reserve were hard to procure, guides were in short supply, and there were almost no tourist comforts to be found anywhere nearby. In fact, when I first arrived in 1992, most of what the people I met in villages to the south and west of the Ankarana massif knew of foreign interest in the reserve came from their observations of, and the rumours surrounding, two foreign-led research projects in the 1980s. Internationally, these projects became known through the findings and documentaries that signalled the rediscovery of Ankarana's distinctive biodiversity and ecosystems (see Wilson, Stewart, and Fowler 1988, for example). Locally, however, these projects were known for the foreigners they involved, people who spent months camped out in forest clearings that were eventually named for their founders: "the campsite of the Americans" and "the campsite of the English." Just what it was that these Americans, English, and their Malagasy associates were looking for in, and taking out of, the reserve's forests and caves was little known to people in the region. All that any I spoke with were certain of was that it must have been worth a great deal to them. Why else would they have put up with the hardships of life in the forest for months at a time? The rumour I heard most often was that they were after mercury—a natural resource that I was assured was both plentiful inside the reserve and of great value to foreigners. Indeed, when I first arrived in the region, more than one person welcomed me by offering to show me the way to sites where they claimed this resource could be found, assuming that I had been sent to the region to follow up on the work of my fellow anglophones.

Research projects of the sort described above were common in Madagascar in the 1980s. In addition to bringing international attention to the island's great biodiversity, they raised international concern over the future of this biodiversity and, more specifically, over the threat posed to it by Malagasy people. This concern resulted in the creation of Madagascar's National Environmental Action Plan (NEAP)—a plan developed in 1991, and then implemented in three phases over the next 17 years, by the Malagasy government, international lenders, foreign aid agencies, and environmental non-governmental organizations. The plan's central purpose was to "reconcile" Madagascar's population "with its environment in order to achieve sustainable development" (cited in Pollini 2011: 76)—to try to ensure, in other words, that the island's ongoing "development" would not come at the cost of losing its distinctive biodiversity. And no business appeared to have more potential in promoting both development and biodiversity conservation simultaneously in Madagascar than ecotourism—a niche of the multibillion-dollar international tourism industry that was then just coming into its own.

The authors of Madagascar's NEAP weren't the only ones to celebrate the great promise of ecotourism during the 1990s. For many planners and observers around the world, ecotourism had come to be seen as a potential "magic bullet" (Brockington, Duffy, and Igoe 2008: 136), offering a means for solving "the dilemma of conserving nature while achieving short-term economic gains" (Krüger 2005: 579) for people on whom the long-term economic costs of conservation were bound to be the greatest—that is, people who would lose access to land, building material, fuel, and other important local resources located inside newly protected areas (see, for example, Ferraro 2002). The promise of ecotourism couldn't have been simpler or more compelling: here was a means, many supposed, for giving a distinctive kind of economic value to endangered environments and, consequently, incentives for conserving them. If all goes according to plan, the outcome of ecotourism ought to be win-win-win: ecotourists ought to win by getting to experience the "natural areas" that attract them, people living alongside such "natural areas" ought to win through opportunities for work enabled by the presence of wealthy outsiders in their midst, and those interested in the protection of these natural areas ought to win as everyone else involved becomes invested in the mission of conservation.

I attended several public meetings in 1993 and 1994 at which much was made of the promise of ecotourism in Ankarana. Even the Antankarana ruler promoted the possibilities represented by an anticipated flood of wealthy foreigners into the region, proposing that people in the village in which I was living ought to be building huts that could be rented to visitors, weaving mats and baskets that could be sold to them, and learning French and English (from me) in anticipation of their arrival. He even commissioned plans for renovating the ceremonial palace in this village and for building a museum alongside it under the assumption that foreign visitors would be just as interested in local culture and history as they were in the region's forests and caves. Optimism was in the air, and based on what I knew at the time, there was good reason to be optimistic.

By the mid-1990s, Ankarana's international reputation as a place of spectacular natural wonders was already well founded. The massif and its caves had been featured in several nature documentaries and magazine profiles seen in Europe and North America, and in 1994 the Ankarana Reserve made a greatly hyped appearance in a documentary produced by Jacques Cousteau, the famed French oceanographer and TV personality. Just as important from the perspective of ecotourism's national and international promoters, however, was the reserve's favourable location, just west of the national highway running between the city of Antsiranana and a port facing the island of Nosy Be. Any international travellers arriving in either of these already popular tourist destinations would have no trouble fitting a visit to Ankarana into a tour of the region, provided, of course, that the reserve's natural wonders could be made accessible to them.

In an effort to streamline visitor access to Ankarana's attractions, a management office was established in Mahamasina, at a spot on the national highway where an old logging road ran into the middle of the reserve. This place shortly became the primary entrance to the reserve and, as such, the local centre of Ankarana's ecotourist trade. Here, visitors could get easy access not only to the reserve's central attractions, but also to the permits, guides, lodging, and supplies necessary for a visit. With funds and other assistance made available through the NEAP, an interpretive centre was built, and new attractions, trails, and circuits were developed—all to better serve foreign visitors. New businesses sprang up as well. By the early 2000s, Mahamasina offered visitors several shops at which they might buy water, snacks, batteries, toilet paper, and other necessities, as well as hotels and restaurants at which they could find a cold drink, a hot meal, and a comfortable bed after a long day of hiking. Such developments pointed to a certain kind of success, as did the increasing numbers of foreign visitors with which they were associated. In the early 1990s, the Ankarana Reserve received fewer than 2,000 foreign visitors per year; in 2008, almost 10,000 foreigners visited what had by then been renamed Ankarana National Park.

The trends described above were not exclusive to Ankarana. Ecotourism's increasing popularity among planners and travellers was a global phenomenon, reaching an important milestone when the United Nations declared 2002 the "year of ecotourism" (Krüger 2005). In Madagascar specifically, visitor arrivals rose from 53,000 in 1990 to 160,000 in 2000 (Duffy 2006: 133) and then to 345,000 by 2008 (Freudenberger 2010: 24), increasing numbers of them coming specifically to visit conservation areas that had been promoted and made more accessible under the auspices of the NEAP. While some celebrated this growth as proof of ecotourism's previously unrealized potential, others were more cautious. Researchers, in particular, used the opportunity afforded by ecotourism's rapid growth in Madagascar and around the world to investigate how well this industry had been able to live up to its reputation as a means for enabling win-win-win scenarios. Findings differed considerably depending both on the cases considered and on the perspectives and priorities of researchers, but what comes across clearly in the great majority of the hundreds of case studies produced since the early 1990s is that the promise of ecotourism is never realized in the simple ways imagined by the industry's promoters (Krüger 2005). Even in and around popular ecotourist destinations like Ankarana National Park, the actual benefits of ecotourism have tended not to live up to the promise that preceded them.

There is no doubt that ecotourism has brought benefits to some people living around Ankarana National Park, most obviously to Mahamasina's Malagasy entrepreneurs, hotel workers, shop-owners, guides, porters, and others working directly or indirectly in the service of foreign visitors. The problem is that the majority of these several dozen people are *not*, in fact, originally from the communities in the immediate vicinity of the park. They are, instead, people from throughout the region (and country) whose capital, skills, knowledge, connections, and experience brought them to this place in search of opportunities opened up by the establishment of the easily accessed park entrance at the side of the highway. For others living in communities on less accessible fringes of the park, meanwhile, the fact that the region's ecotourist trade has become centralized in Mahamasina has made it hard to envision how they might ever benefit from the wealthy foreign visitors that Ankarana's natural wonders have been pulling in. Not even the Antankarana ruler's now 20-year-old plan for a renovated palace and museum has ever been realized. The village in which these attractions are meant to be located is 17 kilometres from the main highway and accessible by car only during the driest times of the year—not at all the kind of place that would be easy for an ecotourist (or a guide from outside of the region) to find, let alone fit into a week-long tour of the region.

Those implementing Madagascar's Environmental Action Plan had anticipated that the direct benefits of ecotourism in regions like Ankarana would be limited, so they instituted a means by which a portion of the entrance fees paid by foreign visitors would go to funding small development projects in communities surrounding particular protected areas (Durbin and Ratrimoarisaona 1996). Around Ankarana, such projects have included health clinics, new school buildings, and a community library. Demand for such funds has always been far greater than supply, and no number of projects is likely to change the common local perception that ecotourism benefits outsiders much more than it does local people. And this perception is not just sour grapes. The truth is that ecotourism in Ankarana *has* mostly benefitted people with little connection to the region.

From the very start of the global ecotourism boom, critics pointed out, as Bandy put it, that "the flourishing [international] ecotourism industry ... benefited travel agencies and tour operators of overdeveloped countries significantly more than the local governments and peoples of" countries like Madagascar (1996: 553). Twenty years into the boom, not much has changed. Indeed, a recent study of tourist preferences and behaviour around several protected areas in Madagascar suggests that less than 10 per cent of a visitor's budget is likely to go to fees and services in these locations (Wollenberg et al. 2011: 105). In Ankarana, as in other ecotourist destinations, the cost of "getting there" has always been far greater than any costs incurred while actually there, and those who benefit most from getting ecotourists to the places they want to see are the airlines, travel agents, and tour operators to whom places like Ankarana National Park are little more than bait. Some national and international tour operators have cultivated relationships with, and contracted services out to, Mahamasina's guides and other local service providers. Most have not, however, preferring to retain as much control and profit as they can by training and paying their own guides to meet the specific demands of their clientele (Jensen 2009). In Ankarana, several foreign tour operators have even built their own eco-lodges in which their clients can drink, eat, and sleep away from the bustle of Mahamasina, and at a much higher cost. These tour operators do not view ecotourism in the way that planners who celebrate this industry's promise do. For tour operators, ecotourism is not primarily a means for ensuring sustainable development in regions like Ankarana, but, rather, a business. And as in any business in which viability depends on the reliability of associates, they risk a lot when deciding to trust local guides and hotel owners to meet their clients' expectations (Jensen 2009: 138). For tour operators, there is little to be gained, and much to be lost, in trying to engineer winning scenarios for local people.

What about the future? Could it not be that ecotourism has simply not yet achieved its promise? As with any business, ecotourism in Ankarana will grow only to the extent that its client base does. And although such growth might generate more park fees, and thus has the potential to produce more funding for small development projects in communities surrounding the park, it will bring problems as well. Research on the industry has shown that "higher tourist numbers" in regions like Ankarana "have been accompanied by lower 'yields' (expenditures) per tourist" (Freudenberger 2010: 71); the more visitors who come, in other words, the less each is likely to spend in the region. Still, as long as there are more visitors each year, and all pay park fees, surely this is a good thing? Not necessarily. For reasons to be fully explored in the next chapter, the sustainability of ecotourism projects depends in large part on maintaining their main attractions as apparently "pristine" and "undisturbed"; *too many* visitors, in other words, can pose just as big a threat to the long-term viability of sustainable ecotourism in a region as can *not enough* visitors. Indeed, in a recent overview of ecotourism projects around the world, Krüger notes how easy it is for "successful ecotourism projects [to] ... fall victim to their own success" (2005: 593) in this way. One proposed solution to this dilemma in Madagascar is that ecotourist destinations might do better to attract fewer and "higher end visitors" (Freudenberger 2010: 71) with more money to spend per capita. Fewer fee-paying visitors in Ankarana would mean a smaller pot of money to share with local communities, however, and "higher end visitors" tend to expect a quality of comfort and service that is more likely to be found at foreign-owned eco-lodges than in the hotels of Mahamasina's entrepreneurs.

Increasing numbers of visitors to Ankarana National Park is also likely to have negative effects on the very biodiversity and ecosystems that this protected area was meant to be protecting in the first place. Not only have new ecotourism developments around protected areas been shown to have "indirect effects" (Duffy 2002: 61; 2010) on endangered environments around the world, but increasing numbers of visitors *within* these areas can have negative effects as well. In Ankarana National Park, increasing visitor numbers have unquestionably had impacts on local ecosystems. Around one campsite I visited in 2010, for example, crowned lemurs have become

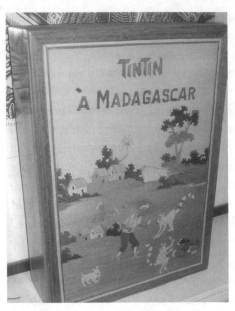
A souvenir featuring Tintin as a lemur-feeding tourist.

so accustomed to being fed by visitors that they now approach new arrivals with no fear. Whatever such a change in behaviour portends for the survival of this species, there is no doubt as to what it indicates about the rule-breaking visitors who have been feeding them.

Indeed, we mustn't forget that it is ecotourists themselves who are arguably the greatest beneficiaries of Ankarana's ecotourism industry. At least *they* seem to be getting what they've been promised in the brochures that draw them to this place, close encounters with crowned lemurs included. In the next section I discuss the motivations and demands of Ankarana's ecotourists further by considering the work and perspectives of those who have come to know them best—the Malagasy guides who lead them through Ankarana National Park.

The Practice of Ecotourism in Ankarana

Driving into Mahamasina, the first people you are likely to see working in the region's ecotourist trade appear not to be working at all. These are the guides, park employees, local hotel owners, and drivers who congregate around a bench just off the main road, playing dominoes, talking, and waiting for new visitors to arrive. On my first full day in Mahamasina in 2004, I spent an hour in conversation with several of these men. A driver in the group had just returned from dropping off a load of visitors at a campsite inside the park, and he was in a complaining mood. Although he didn't own the 4×4 he drove, he was the one responsible for its maintenance, and the more trips he took on this bad road, he said, the more damage it caused the vehicle, and the more likely that he would get yelled at by the foreign tour operator he worked for. A park employee seated with us countered that since it was tour operators, like the driver's employer, who most commonly used the park's road, and since it was their large 4×4s and minibuses that had caused most of the damage, perhaps *they* should pay for repairs; given budgetary constraints, the park's management was certainly in no position to pave the road, as the driver had suggested might be a possibility. Back and forth it went for several rounds until the two guides seated with us intervened and put an end to the debate with their own expert observations. You can't repair these roads too well, one of them stated matter-of-factly. However much tourists might complain about the bumps and jolts that come with the ride into the park, they would complain even more if they saw asphalt within its boundaries. It just wouldn't be "*naturel*," the second guide added, using a French term for which there is no clear Malagasy equivalent. The driver acknowledged the point, adding that a paved road would likely result in increased tourist traffic inside the park, something that his passengers would be sure to complain about.

After only an hour on this bench, I knew I had found a place where I might learn a great deal about the practice of ecotourism in Ankarana. The guides, guards, entrepreneurs, drivers, and others who regularly gathered here were experts on this topic, and for good reason. Whereas the majority of ecotourists I have met in Ankarana over the years were "once in a lifetime" visitors to the region, these men—and they were mostly men—had spent years dealing regularly with foreign visitors. And of these experts, none knew more about the complex motivations and interests of ecotourists than the guides who led them through Ankarana National Park. What was short-term recreation to ecotourists was a livelihood for their guides, and there was no doubt as to who had spent more time thinking critically, as an anthropologist might, about the business that had brought them together here. In recognition of this fact, the following discussion of the practice of ecotourism in Ankarana is organized largely around the work and insights of one such guide.

Like most of the guides who worked regularly in Mahamasina in 2004, Robert did not come originally from the immediate vicinity of Ankarana National Park. He was born, rather, on the island of Nosy Be, about 200 kilometres southwest of Ankarana, where he was raised amidst the bustle of the "mass tourism," "beach tourism," and "sex tourism" for which this long-popular destination has come to be very well known internationally. Obviously, the kind of tourism that occupied Robert in Mahamasina in 2004 was in many ways quite different to that with which he grew up. Indeed, ecotourism has often been promoted as a more sustainable and ethical alternative to the sort on display in Nosy Be's beachfront resorts and nightclubs.

Robert and other guides knew better than to draw too sharp a distinction between one kind of visitor to Madagascar and another, however; visitors to Ankarana National Park couldn't always be counted on to live up to the reputations that preceded them. In fact, given the park's location alongside a highway that runs between the nightclubs of Antsiranana and the beaches of Nosy Be, it wasn't unusual for Robert to see and work for the kind of tourists with whom he had grown up. For him, the subtle distinctions that some observers suggest ought to be drawn between different categories of tourists didn't matter as much as the simple and obvious distinction between all of these outsiders and people in Madagascar—they were all *vazaha*, or "foreigners," the generic term commonly used to refer to any non-Malagasy visitors to the park.

In the mid-1990s, Robert travelled from Nosy Be to Madagascar's capital of Antananarivo with the intention of studying English at the national university. Drawn to the opportunities presented by the country's newly booming ecotourist industry, he eventually enrolled in a program at one of the capital's newly founded private tourism-training institutes and then got a job, through family connections, as a driver with a foreign-owned tour company that specialized in taking groups to popular beach and ecotourist destinations in the far south of the island. This work taught him more English (as well as French and German) than he would ever learn at university. His language training didn't stop there, however. Aware of how important language skills were to the work of guiding, he spent much of his down time in Mahamasina poring over a tattered notebook in which he had written phonetic versions of foreign vocabulary and phrases he had collected from clients. Along with several other guides in Mahamasina, he had also taken up learning to speak Italian in recent years, following the opening of an Italian-owned beach resort nearby. Robert insisted that he wanted to do more than speak these languages—he wanted to understand them, not just so that he could converse with his clients but also so that he could comprehend what they were saying to one another. Like other guides, he was concerned that clients might use their native languages to criticize him, and recognized that even a little competency in a foreign language could be a deterrent.

Robert moved to Mahamasina in the late 1990s. Although he brought years of experience in Madagascar's tourist trade with him, he still had more to learn. To earn the licence that would enable him to guide in Ankarana National Park, he was required to complete a training course and qualifying exam overseen by the park's management. Therefore, he joined other prospective guides in learning about the distinctive flora, fauna, and geological features that he would be encountering in the region, as well as the many regulations that he and his clients would be required to follow while inside the park. This training also gave him an introduction to the idea of Ankarana as a sacred cultural landmark and familiarized him with the history and taboos that have made and keep it so. As someone who didn't grow up in the region, however, Robert never professed to be a specialist in local history or culture, remarking to me that I probably knew more than he did. Indeed, as much as he and other guides I met in 2004 would make note of the English translations of words and expressions they asked me to teach them, they also took great interest in anything I could tell them about the history and ceremonies that connected Antankarana people to the Ankarana massif, knowing that I had done research on topics that some of their clients might be interested in learning about.

In the early years of the region's ecotourism boom, young men and women who self-identified as Antankarana were encouraged to earn the qualifications necessary for working as guides in the region. Several of them did so, assuming, as planners had, that their familiarity with the region and its history would give them certain advantages over relative outsiders like Robert. The work of guiding foreign visitors requires more than just knowing one's way around a particular place, however. Whatever advantages Antankarana candidates had because of their familiarity with local landscapes, history, and taboos were offset for most of them by an insurmountable lack of other necessary qualifications: in particular, specialist education, language skills, and previous experience with foreigners. Today, relatively few of the guides certified to lead visitors through Ankarana National Park would ever claim to be "of Ankarana." Other guides who did consider themselves Antankarana preferred to base themselves in the city of Antsiranana, from where they can lead visitors on tours in northern Madagascar that might or might not include stops in Ankarana National Park.

One of the most lucrative forms of work for qualified guides like Robert was provided by foreign conservation biologists, zoologists, primatologists, and others doing research in the region. Although these scientists were rightly concerned about the effects that increasing numbers of visitors were having on the region's distinctive biodiversity and ecosystems (see, for example, Cardiff et al. 2009), the emergence of Ankarana National Park as a popular ecotourist destination had not dampened their interest in what the place had to offer. If anything, Mahamasina's emergence as a convenient site in which to find guides, accommodations, and supplies had made doing research inside the National Park easier, and less expensive, than ever. Not long before I met him, Robert had spent several weeks with a pair of Australian graduate students who were trying to track and monitor the behaviour of a particular species of lemur in Ankarana. Shortly after I left him in 2004, he was scheduled to spend three weeks with another researcher intent on photographing the reserve's wildlife. Such work paid well, but it involved certain sacrifices. Working with researchers generally involved long days of walking and, sometimes, hauling equipment around, and often meant living in tents inside the park, eating the same food day after day, and taking on cooking as well as guiding duties. In other words, such work wasn't for everybody; as Robert noted, some of Mahamasina's guides "don't even have tents!" For those who did do this kind of work, however, it was more than just the possibility of weeks or months of steady pay that attracted them. All guides should have "specialties," Robert told me, whether bats, birds, lemurs, insects, reptiles, plants or whatever. And the best way to develop the expertise needed to claim such specialties was through work with foreign researchers. By 2004, Robert claimed several specialties of his own, though he was still waiting for the chance to work with a geologist so that he might become a specialist in the region's caves as well.

As should be clear by now, the work of guiding was itself a distinctive specialty that guides like Robert worked hard to develop by enrolling in training programs, studying foreign languages, and, sometimes, assisting foreign researchers. The knowledge gained through such self-directed learning could take them only so far in mitigating the risks of this uncertain trade, however. Robert could never be sure what a day would bring. Since most visitors to the park arrived without prior notice, he had to wait his turn behind other qualified guides for opportunities to work. He might end up with an individual client intent on three days of hiking, or with a group interested in just a morning or afternoon at attractions accessible in their own car. Or he might spend a day waiting in vain. When he did get clients, his pay was regular—the equivalent of around $20 per day—and with a week of steady work he could earn more than a park guard stationed elsewhere in the region made in a month. Guiding work was seasonal, however, meaning that Robert had to squeeze in as much of it as he could between July and October when most foreigners travel to the region; an injury, illness or other setback during peak season could ruin his year, as, of course, could events beyond his control. Robert had already struggled through the *crise* of 2002—a national political crisis that resulted in a dramatic dip in the number of foreign visitors to Madagascar—and within a few years of our time together he was destined to struggle through another in 2009, a point to which I will return in the Conclusion.

Robert found some security in the good relationship he had developed with a Dutch tour company that paid him twice his regular guiding rate over 15 days every year to lead one of their groups on a standard tour of northern Madagascar. As noted in the previous section, however, most tour operators brought their own guides with them to Ankarana, and although they were required to hire a local guide in Mahamasina if none of their own employees had completed the aforementioned qualification program, their total contribution to the local ecotourist trade was minimal. Most guides in Mahamasina, certainly, would much rather have seen five pairs of independent visitors seeking five different guides arrive than the meagre prospect of a minibus of 10 package-tour visitors travelling with an outside guide of their own—even if, as several guides told me, independent backpackers tended to tip less and wanted to hike more than visitors travelling in groups. Similarly, local hotel owners saw no benefit in groups that stayed in foreign-owned eco-lodges.

Robert had also developed good relationships with many of his own clients over the years. As he saw it, being friendly, understanding, and approachable mattered almost as much in the trade as being knowledgeable. He had friends "all over the world," he told me, and he had postcards, photos, and a pair of gifted hiking boots to prove it. And he wasn't alone. Other guides in Mahamasina had mementos of their own—photos of themselves sharing meals with former clients, for example, or T-shirts that had been given as souvenirs of time spent together. From what I observed of visitor–guide relations, visitors shared meals, photos, and souvenirs with guides not as acts of commerce or charity, but as acts of social intimacy that enabled them to leave, as well as take away, evidence of the personal connections they had made in this place.

The more time I spent with Robert and other guides in Mahamasina in 2004, the more their work and lives seemed akin to those of the sapphire miners and traders with whom I had been spending time in previous years. Like Ambondromifehy's miners and traders, the guides I interviewed in Mahamasina had gotten into the ecotourist trade as prospectors, risking the uncertainties of a fickle business in the hope that it would pay off for them in the way they had seen it pay off for others. Neither guides nor sapphire workers had come to Ankarana with the intention of settling permanently; Robert was certainly as mobile as any of the miners or traders discussed in the previous chapter, and he was ready to leave when necessary. Furthermore, while the kinds of experience and knowledge that Mahamasina's guides sought and valued so highly were clearly different from those preoccupying Ambondromifehy's miners and traders, all shared a keen awareness of the significance of this experience and knowledge to the success they were after. Indeed, it was this experience and knowledge that any of them would take away with them if they left the region to practise their trades elsewhere on the island. What was most similar of all about Mahamasina's guides and Ambondromifehy's miners and traders, however, was the simple fact that all had been drawn to the region to work in trades dedicated ultimately to fulfilling the demands of foreign consumers. And in this respect, Mahamasina's guides clearly had an important advantage. Where sapphire miners and traders living up the road went about their work with little awareness of the specific interests and motivations of the ultimate consumers of the sapphires coming out of Ankarana, Mahamasina's guides were fully immersed in the distinctive demands and motivations of their clients.

Ankarana National Park does not attract only one kind of foreign visitor, Robert told me. Visitors arrived by bush taxi, minibus, 4×4, car, or bicycle. Some brought tents and wanted to camp in the forest; others were happy to stay in one of the inexpensive lodging complexes outside the park. Some complained about the din of the generator and TV in one of Mahamasina's restaurants; others considered the music videos and action movies shown on this TV, and the local children they gathered, to be glimpses of local colour. Inside the reserve, visitors were no less diverse. Some expected their guides to be silent; others preferred to chat and responded well to guides' attempts at humour. Some wanted to see all of the wildlife that the park had to offer; others were happy just to hang out in their campsite, "taking in the breeze," as guides would say of them. Some visitors wanted to keep moving; others were pleased with every new game of "spot the reptile" in which a guide would stop to point them in the general direction of a camouflaged chameleon or uroplatus and have them try to find it. Visitors could also sometimes be "poorly behaved," as Robert put it, transgressing park rules by shining lights on sleeping bats, feeding lemurs, and trampling off-trail into areas from which they were meant to be restricted. Although guides were expected to discourage such behaviour, and to report it to park management when it took place, doing so could put someone like Robert in an awkward position. Reporting a client might cost him a day's tip, or, in some cases, endanger his reputation among outside tour operators.

Signs indicating different paths that visitors to Ankarana National Park can follow.

To hear Robert speak of it, his work in Ankarana had done more than just supply him with an income. It had led to the sort of transformation that promoters of ecotourism promise is possible. As a child, he told me, he had no respect for plants or animals. Meeting and working with foreign researchers and tourists over the years, however, had changed him into a conservationist; indeed, he told me that he cared more about the great biodiversity found in Ankarana National Park than most of his clients did. He had even developed a special fondness for the most "bizarre," as he put it, of Ankarana's reptiles: the uroplatus, a type of gecko. "If I don't see a uroplatus [on a trip into the park]," he told me, "I am not at ease. It's only when I see one that I can be at ease ... even if the tourists don't care, it is important to me to see this reptile."

No matter how uninterested or "poorly behaved" foreign visitors might sometimes be, as far as Robert was concerned there was no merit in comparing their impact on the park with that caused by others in the region. "Ankarana" he told me, "is really in danger," and, as he saw it, sapphire mining was the biggest reason. Sapphire miners, he explained,

> come in [to the park] and cut trees ... they kill lemurs, they do all sorts of things. And here [inside the park] there are especially attractive tourist destinations ... the *tsingy* [limestone pinnacles] and the caves ... these are very important. ... it's all saddening.

A year earlier, Robert had come upon a group of four miners starting a pit not far from a path leading to a seldom-visited attraction in the park. He threatened to report them to park officials back in Mahamasina, and warned them that police would be returning shortly to arrest them. Thankfully, he said, the foreign visitors who were with him on that trip didn't see the miners, and when they asked him about the pits, he told them that this was a hole dug by animals during the rainy season; he assumed that news of mining inside the park would either frighten or anger his clients. Like other guides and conservation workers who complained about sapphire mining inside the park, Robert was clearly concerned about more than just the threat that this activity posed to conservation. As he saw it, mining also posed a threat to the ultimate source of his living—that is, the sensibilities of foreign visitors who expected to find the park in pristine condition.

Abandoned mining pits weren't the only signs of illegal activity that Robert encountered inside the park—he also witnessed the sight of stone cairns left behind by herders in search of grazing cattle, the smell of smoke from smoldering charcoal pits, and the sound of axes on trees destined for furniture makers in a nearby town. The land around Mahamasina was originally settled during the colonial era by cattle herders, and in 2004 people living just down the road from the Park entrance continued to subsist largely from raising cattle, farming rice, and, occasionally, producing charcoal, lumber or gravel for sale to people in nearby towns. Robert's concern over the activities of these neighbours, however, was tempered by an awareness of their circumstances. "It's very difficult [to make a living] here" he told me, referring to the case of a man he knew down the road:

> How many people have been found making charcoal here? But what are you going to do when you live in the same community [as these charcoal producers]? Are you going to lock them up? When you see their children and their wife there? How are you going to lock them up?

As Sodikoff (2009) has argued was the case among guides and other conservation workers around Masoala National Park in northeastern Madagascar, Robert was in the awkward position of living alongside people whose illegal activities appeared to be endangering the conservation efforts with which his own livelihood and emerging conservationist ethos were so closely tied. Unlike the conservation workers Sodikoff describes, however, whose livelihoods were still largely tied to landscapes shared with these neighbours, Robert always had the option, and sometimes the desire, to leave

Mahamasina. Moving on to another ecotourist destination on the island might require that he complete a new training and certification program, but wherever he might go, he would take with him the kind of knowledge most essential for succeeding in Madagascar's ecotourism industry: notebooks filled with foreign vocabulary, contacts developed through work with foreign researchers and tour operators, and invaluable experience gained from years of leading clients through one of the island's many National Parks.

Speculating about Ecotourism in Ankarana

As noted at the beginning of the previous section, what drew me to Robert and other guides I spent time with in 2004 was that they had already studied what I myself had come to Mahamasina to study; for reasons that should be clear by now, they had made themselves experts on ecotourism. That their knowledge of the trade was based not just on observation but on *participant*-observation—that is, on having simultaneously participated in and observed it—made their understandings even more appealing; participant-observation is a method that anthropologists have long celebrated as an invaluable means for generating insights into complex phenomena like this one. Prior to 2004, most of what I had heard about ecotourism in Ankarana had come from people in the region who had only ever *observed* it from a distance—sapphire miners like the ones Robert had shooed out of the park, for example, or traders in Ambondromifehy who would try to sell sapphires to the foreigners who stopped in town on their way to Mahamasina. And, as noted at the end of the previous chapter, the speculations of these observers supported nothing more concrete than rumours of the sort I had been hearing since I first came to the region in the early 1990s: that foreigners were after mercury, bones, sapphires or something else that they were intending to take *out* of the Ankarana massif.

Rumours like these bothered Robert, as did accompanying rumours about people like him. As he told me during one of our last conversations in 2004, other Malagasy people would often ask him, "What is the meaning of the visits of those *vazaha* [foreigners]?" "We've heard that there are sapphires and mercury inside [the park]," they would say. "That's not true!," Robert would answer.

> We try our hardest to make [people who ask such things] understand. We tell them that when tourists come, they learn the rules: to leave only

footprints, and take only photos. We tell them that they come here to see the land, to see things that they don't have where they are from, to see chameleons, to see animals, just that.

Other local participant-observers of ecotourism offered similar accounts of conversations with puzzled neighbours, friends, and relatives. Anne, a park employee, described another:

There was an elder relative of mine [who] asked me "Hey, my child, what is the reason for the visits of these *vazaha* ... why is it that they have come?" I laughed. "Do you want to know the reason for their visits? They come to see chameleons. They come to see lizards. Half of them come to see ants. Some come to see birds, and then there are some who come to see only trees." "Is that so!?!," he said. "Ya!," I said. "Haaa! Kakakakaka!" He almost fainted he was laughing so hard. ... "Really my daughter!?!" ... [He said,] "I was thinking that there were sapphires there, I thought there was gold there ... but that is all they are here to see?" [I answered] "Ya ... they come to see animals, to see snakes." He laughed and laughed.

Anne and Robert agreed that the best hope for dispelling rumours about foreigners visiting the park was the same approach that had long been used to encourage residents of Ankarana to respect the park's rules and boundaries: namely *sensibilisation*, a French term commonly used to describe education and awareness-raising programs concerning the goals and value of conservation efforts in the region. If only local residents could see, and would believe, why foreigners were *really* interested in Ankarana National Park, the thinking went, they might come to value the place differently (in the way that Robert had) and maybe even embrace the goals of conservation themselves.

Over the years, I too have encountered many questions and rumours about foreigners visiting Ankarana National Park, never so often as when I found myself in Ambondromifehy. In 1999, for example, I heard many stories of the suspicious behaviour of foreign visitors: of *vazaha* entering caves and not emerging for hours, of Malagasy porters hauling heavy bags out of the park, and of 4×4s being unloaded of so much baggage and equipment that they could only have belonged to foreign sapphire prospectors.

From the perspective of Ambondromifehy's speculators, there was no doubt about the role played by the foreign and national conservation agencies that managed the park. What these organizations really conserved,

A minibus-load of tourists stopped in Ambondromifehy.

many assumed, was the exclusive access of foreigners to the resources they desired; indeed, some reasoned that this was why the entrance at Mahamasina had been improved only a few years before Malagasy prospectors' discovery of sapphires in the park. Some speculators even guessed that the park's managers helped to regulate the various claims of different foreign powers. One miner cited the names of the park's oldest campsites—the "campsite of the Americans" and the "campsite of the English"—as proof of such competing foreign claims. To him, the fact that these campsites had subsequently been given Malagasy names was not, as I had suggested, a sign of efforts at emphasizing the fact that the park was under Malagasy management; as he saw it, these name changes were signs of a cover-up.

When I returned to Ambondromifehy for a short visit in 2004, rumours about foreigners continued to circulate, and speculators argued away my assurances that foreign visitors to the park do, as Anne and Robert had said, "come to see chameleons" and to "take only pictures." If they come here just to see chameleons, a miner asked me rhetorically, why must they do so in a "protected area" that also happens to have sapphires? Chameleons are just as plentiful outside of the park, he assured me, on the other side of the highway, where sapphires *can't* be found. A trader sitting with us added that while the foreigners *I* had been observing over the previous weeks might be taking only pictures, they were probably doing so for reasons I hadn't been able to discern—maybe, he speculated, these pictures were destined for distant prospectors who wanted evidence of what the park had to offer before coming themselves.

By contrast, all of those I interviewed who lived alongside the park entrance in Mahamasina had come to accept that the foreigners who visited the park *were*, in fact, interested mostly in chameleons and taking pictures. This didn't stop them from speculating, however. Several assumed that the photographs foreigners took would eventually be sold to others; this was why, one woman proposed, foreign visitors came with special medicines that attracted the animals they wanted to photograph. In another interview, an elder named Nivo—a man who lived less than 100 metres from the park entrance—speculated as to why foreign visitors to Ankarana used mosquito repellent: "They don't want you to kill mosquitoes," he explained, referring to personal experiences with foreigners in the past.

> If they see you kill one, they'll get upset. They have their mosquito repellent ... and they spray it on you so that the mosquitoes will stay away, and you won't kill them.

As Nivo saw it, the conservationist zeal of foreign visitors to Ankarana was so great that it trumped all else as an explanation for their willingness to share mosquito repellent—not so far-fetched a possibility, it should be noted, in a place in which foreigners often do show great interest in insects. Although Nivo was among those in Mahamasina who assured me that the foreigners who visited Ankarana National Park were *not* interested in extracting sapphires or mercury from the place, he was also aware that these visitors viewed the region's natural resources (mosquitoes included) in their own distinctive way: "I don't see what foreigners see when they go walking in the forest," he concluded.

Given Nivo's comments, some might be inclined to emphasize cultural differences in making sense of the rumours and speculations proposed by those in the region who had only ever had the chance to *observe* foreign visitors. If Ankarana's speculators simply "don't see what foreigners see" in Ankarana National Park, it isn't surprising that they can't fathom why such foreigners would ever want to travel halfway around the world to "take only pictures" of what they see there. A long-standing premise of environmental anthropology is that people "see," value, and interact with environments differently and in learned ways, and there is clearly some element of the way in which foreigners value "what they see when they go walking in the forest" in Ankarana that can be learned—something that Robert, Anne, and other Malagasy advocates of conservation in Mahamasina claimed to have learned through their work in the local ecotourist trade.

The main problem with an argument that emphasizes cultural differences in trying to explain, or resolve, the conflicts of interpretation and interest that have developed around Ankarana National Park in recent decades is that it distracts from far more obvious aspects of the situation at hand. Anthropologists and other participant-observers can easily become so taken with the task of investigating what is *not* obvious about phenomena under consideration, and then so intent on communicating that there is "more than meets the eye" (Rappaport 1979) in what others are misinterpreting, that it is easy for us to lose sight of what *is*, in fact, obvious to *any* observer. What Mahamasina's and Ambondromifehy's speculating observers understood perfectly well from observation alone, for example, was that it was more than just distinctive desires and motivations that brought foreigners to Ankarana, and more than just what they "see when they go walking in the forest" that accounted for their presence inside Ankarana National Park.

Toward the end of the interview in which Nivo speculated about foreigners' use of mosquito repellent, I asked him why it is that foreigners would travel to Ankarana to walk in the forest, see animals, or "take in the breeze" here when they might do these things in National Parks or zoos at home. His answer was simple: "They have enough money to do it!" he exclaimed. He explained further:

> ... dollars and French francs and Malagasy francs aren't the same. 50 French francs becomes what, 50 000 Malagasy francs? How could they not have enough money to fulfill all of their desires? They exchange 100 of their francs and they get enough to do whatever they want ... they get a rice sack full of money. They have enough money, I said! We are different. Our money is *boozaka* ... [the grass used] to make the roof of your hut.

What kind of an explanation of ecotourism is this? Certainly not the kind I was expecting when I asked the question. Instead of hearing Nivo's reflections on foreign values and motivations, what I got was the obvious: foreigners come to Ankarana because they *can*.

The perspective from which an obvious point like this is especially meaningful is one that many readers might find hard to appreciate. To give a sense of what I mean by it, then, and of how easily it can be overlooked, consider the following simple thought experiment. Suppose that *you* were asked to explain the presence of foreign visitors in a place like Ankarana. How would you respond? You might well begin, as I did above, by reflecting on the distinctive historically and culturally rooted desires and motivations of these visitors, and then proceed to suggest that a place like Ankarana must offer these people what they are seeking. Now suppose that you were asked to explain why people from Ankarana do not travel to the places from which the foreign visitors they observe come? If you knew anything about Ankarana, Madagascar, and the world, you would most likely answer without too much thought to matters of desire or motivation. Overseas travel is simply not an option for most of the people from Ankarana: Not only do most in the region lack the disposable income that might go to airfare (the cost of a flight from Madagascar to Paris is approximately three times Madagascar's average annual income), but they are also constrained by bureaucracies and exclusionary immigration policies that make getting passports and international visas extremely difficult. It is this latter perspective—one that prioritizes the easily observed capacity for action over the hard-to-discern desires and motivations underlying action—that Ankarana's observers tend to take when making sense of the foreign visitors in their midst. And they take this perspective for the same reason that you or I might when explaining why it is that more people from Ankarana cannot be found vacationing in Niagara Falls: because to do otherwise would be to ignore the obvious. This simple point is one that even Robert would have conceded to. Seated together on the bench near the park entrance one day, practising English at his request, I asked Robert what it was that made foreign visitors to Ankarana different from the Malagasy people they encountered here. "We don't have vacations," he answered.

Wealth was not the only privilege that foreign visitors to Ankarana National Park enjoyed, of course. Just as obvious was their privileged access to the park. It was true that, as Robert and others insisted, Malagasy people were welcome to visit the park; indeed, the fees charged to Malagasy citizens were a fraction of those paid by foreigners. Given that the park had been set up to appeal specifically to foreign visitors with distinctive tastes, however, it isn't clear what they would get out of such a visit. The fact is that many of the region's observers did, already, spend time in the park (mining, making charcoal, and looking for lost cattle, for example), but they did so illegally, and they stood to be punished for their visits. Consequently, even years after park management had been transferred from a foreign to a Malagasy conservation agency, people throughout the region continued to identify Ankarana National Park as a place that had been set aside by and for foreigners. To people in Amondromifehy, nothing made this point more obvious than the juxtaposition of a pair of highway-side signs that stood just north of town when I lived there in 1999. The larger of the two signs—a billboard, set back from the road—welcomed French speakers to the northern boundary of what was then still known as "Ankarana Special Reserve," asking them to "take nothing but photographs and leave nothing but footprints" during their stays in the region. The second sign, much smaller and closer to the ground, was intended for people more likely to be on foot than in 4×4s. It read, simply, "ALA FADY," warning Malagasy speakers to keep out of what they were meant to consider a "TABOO FOREST."

It would be hard to find an image more suggestive than this one of the disparities that inspired the speculators cited in this section. Whatever advances had been made through *sensibilisation* to educate or raise awareness about the significance of Ankarana's biodiversity or the potential benefits that might come from conserving it, there was never any question as to whose interests had led to the creation of a "Special Reserve" in the region in the first place, and whose interests were being served by encouraging some to enter this place and others to keep out. Anyone who suggested otherwise, visiting anthropologists included, was either deluded or complicit.

The Problem with Ecotourism

This chapter has offered several different perspectives on ecotourism in Ankarana: the perspectives of planners and park managers who have seen promise in this new niche of the global tourist industry, the perspectives of guides who have invested a great deal in familiarizing themselves with the foreign consumers whose demands drive this industry, and the perspectives of local observers whose speculations remind us not to overlook the obvious inequalities that make places like Ankarana National Park accessible to the visitors they attract. The reality that comes from the entanglement of these different perspectives is complex, but not so unusual. In fact, the situation I have described here is in many ways similar to those described in other parts of Madagascar and the world—contexts in which so much of the great promise of ecotourism is proving to be unrealizable.

Considering the complexity of any one of these cases, one can't help but wonder how anyone could ever have imagined ecotourism as the "panacea" (Krüger 2005), "magic bullet" (Brockington, Duffy, and Igoe 2008), or "golden egg" (Freudenberger 2010) that some have made it out to be. The international ecotourism industry has certainly produced its share of winners in recent years, but it has also left a good many key people out, especially among those who live alongside the attractions that draw ecotourists in—that is, among people whose well-being was meant to be served by ecotourism in the first place. Considered in retrospect and in light of the specifics of the case at hand, this outcome appears inevitable. How is it, then, that those who have trumpeted the promise of ecotourism over the years didn't see it coming?

One of the features of ecotourism that makes it so alluring to conservation-oriented planners, industry promoters, and ecotourists themselves is that it fits so well with certain ways of thinking about how the global economy *ought* to work—ways of thinking that are commonly associated with the term "neoliberalism" (Harvey 2005), which assert the primacy of market principles and thus celebrate, among other things, the power of wealthy consumers to shape the world through consumption choices. According to such thinking, ecotourism *ought* to work in the way planners promise in that it brings wealthy consumers right to the doorsteps of those who could benefit a great deal from their interest. By neoliberal logic, people in Ankarana of all places *ought* to do especially well in that the ecotourist attractions alongside which they live have certain "comparative advantages" (Duffy 2006: 134) over others that consumers might choose to visit elsewhere; not only does Ankarana National Park feature the charismatic lemurs, spectacular landscapes, and chameleons that are internationally associated with Madagascar's "brand" (Duffy 2006: 134), but it also offers remarkably easy access to these and other endemic natural wonders.

As I have shown in this chapter, ecotourism is anything but an uncomplicated means for connecting rich globe-trotting consumers with local entrepreneurial service providers in ways that make better conservationists of all involved. In fact, foreign visitors to ecotourist destinations are never as easily pegged as some imagine them to be, people living around ecotourist attractions are often poorly positioned to provide these foreign consumers with what they are looking for, and the conservation of endangered environments is rarely the first thing on anyone's mind. Like twenty-first-century neoliberal capitalism more generally, in other words, the international ecotourism industry is far more complex than those who celebrate its promise make it out to be—the principles by which it operates can do as much to exclude and dispossess as to include and empower the people we imagine should benefit from their operation (Harvey 2005).

For the purposes of the larger argument presented in this book, it is worth remembering that the global economy that has given ecotourists such easy access to Ankarana is the same one that imposes such limits on the aspirations of this region's sapphire miners and traders. This is a global bazaar in which, as in all bazaar economies, the complex deliberations and choices of buyers exert a far greater influence than do the efforts of those looking to profit from selling them what they want. Indeed, perhaps the most telling similarity between Ankarana's ecotourist and sapphire trades is the fact that both stand to fall apart as soon as foreign consumers lose interest in what the region has to offer them—a point to which I will return in the Conclusion.

In the late 1990s and early 2000s, Ankarana's speculators didn't know much more about foreign visitors to Ankarana National Park than they did about distant sapphire consumers, but they were certainly right to observe that all of these foreigners were interested in Ankarana as a source of something of great value—a fact that inspired another question that I have often been asked by the region's speculators. How is it, they wonder, that people in Madagascar can be "left behind" despite living amidst resources that foreigners value so highly? In the next chapter, I address this apparent paradox in a way that I think would make sense to Ankarana's speculators. My approach is premised on their own, correct, assumption that what draws foreigners into Ankarana National Park *is*, in fact, the same as what foreign consumers seem to be getting out of the sapphires mined here.

NATURAL WONDERS IN THE GLOBAL BAZAAR

"Squinting, peering, I was drawn into a silken world spun by powers beyond my imagination—a secret whispered just for me ... Call it a signal from the gods, a voice from the heavens, an eruption from hell—epiphany—describe it as you like. I put it thus: at that instant, the sun broke through the clouds, the planets aligned. As I held that sapphire ring in my hand, I witnessed the birth of earth and all creation. I gazed upon Pangaea, saw the continents form, then separate ... the true majesty of mother nature struck me." —*Richard Hughes (2001: 5), an American gemmologist, describing a sapphire mined in Madagascar*

"Wowwww!" —*Louis-Philippe, a Malagasy guide, imitating the reaction of an English-speaking foreign visitor upon seeing Ankarana's tsingy for the first time.*

What is obvious to anyone who lives at the side of the highway around Ambondromifehy and Mahamasina is that foreigners place great value on what can be found inside Ankarana National Park—since the late 1990s, as kilo after kilo of sapphires have been leaving the park on their way to foreign destinations, truck-load after truck-load of foreign visitors have been entering in search of something special. In fact, the idea that Ankarana is the source of something of great value to foreigners is one of the few certainties that Jao, Roby, Madame Fernand, Robert, Nivo, and others discussed in the previous two chapters have taken away from their participation in the global bazaar. And when considered alongside the uncertainties of their lives in the region, this obvious fact presents them with a paradox: How is it that people like them can struggle so much despite living and working so close to what wealthy foreigners value so highly? According to Robert, the guide on whom I focused in the last chapter,

> Madagascar ... is the richest of countries. It has every kind of thing you would want to take ... all kinds of resources ... minerals, shrimp, rice ... all the things you would want to take.

Madagascar is *also* rich in resources that foreigners are willing to pay people like Robert to help them visit on site. And yet, he continued, Malagasy people are perpetually "left behind" in the world they share with such foreigners, "struggling" to get by. How can this be? From Robert's perspective, and as many others in the region see it, the cause of this paradox must be the Malagasy government—or, more specifically, corrupt Malagasy politicians and officials who are commonly portrayed as siphoning off most of the money being generated by the country's mining, ecotourism, and other industries.

The Malagasy state has, in fact, played an important role in the development of the two trades described in the previous two chapters. Malagasy governmental officials and agencies played key parts in the implementation of the country's National Environmental Action Plan (NEAP), for example, and the country's Ministry of Tourism has long promoted ecotourism as holding out great promise for the country. State involvement in the country's gemstone trade has been slower, murkier, and less well planned out (Duffy 2007); in 2003, the Ministry of Energy and Mines consolidated its efforts at managing the exploitation and export of the country's sapphires and other minerals through the Mineral Resources Governance Project (or MRGP)—a project that, like the NEAP, was funded by foreign lenders and aid agencies and intended, ultimately, to encourage "sustainable development" (Duffy 2007: 191) in the country. Among the most revealing products of the MRGP was a glossy information package intended for potential foreign investors, its cover featuring an image of a dazzling green gemstone ring at the centre of an orchid above the title "Madagascar: The real treasure island." Within the package, Madagascar is described as a place "with incredibly varied mineral resources, both known and awaiting discovery," and also a "gift to the earth" that promises spectacular flora and fauna within the protective boundaries of dozens of conservation areas.

While plans like the NEAP and programs like the MRGP clearly show the Malagasy state's interest in making the most of foreign interest in what Madagascar has to offer the world's investors, consumers, and conservationists, they also suggest how limited state control over the fate of these resources really is. Since both the NEAP and the MRGP were funded by international players (the World Bank, USAID, and others) who see the island's best hope for sustainable development as lying in supplying global demand for its natural resources, we must think carefully about who stands to benefit most from efforts at promoting Madagascar as "the real treasure island"—especially given that the foreign investors for whom this image is intended have a wide world of island resource frontiers to choose from: Papua New Guinea, for example, where an "abundance of resources" (IPA n.d.) is promised by the country's Investment Promotion Agency; or Fiji, where, according to the marketing arm of the Fijian Government, "you can trade and invest where paradise is yours" (Investment Fiji n.d.).

The so-called "paradox of plenty" facing people in Ankarana is not uncommon in the world today (Karl 1997); it has most often been described with reference to countries deemed to have fallen victim to what some term the "resource curse" (Ross 1999)—that is, countries whose economic development appears to have been impeded rather than helped along by being rich in natural resources. Popular and academic analyses of the paradox of plenty tend to attribute it, as Robert did, to governmental mismanagement of the great public funds that a country's natural resources have the potential to generate. However, given that neither ecotourism nor the sapphire trade has generated much in the way of public funds in Madagascar—or at least nothing near what national oil companies and contracts with multinational mining corporations have generated for other countries around the world—blaming the Malagasy government for the fact that people in Ankarana haven't benefitted more from the treasure around them would be misguided.

In the next two sections, I suggest that we might better understand the paradox facing people who struggle at the edges of Ankarana's treasure trove as a systemic feature of the global bazaar in which people in this region have become caught up. If we imagine the global economy as a bazaar economy in the sense that Ankarana's speculators do, the paradox of benefitting so little from what foreigners value so much is revealed as the outcome of the means by which the economic value of natural resources is realized in the world today. Much like a hungry miner who brings a sapphire into Ambondromifehy on market day, Madagascar may have much to offer the world, but it also has much to lose through bargaining that, as in any bazaar economy, always favour buyers with other choices over sellers with immediate needs.

The approach I take here hinges on the idea that Ankarana's sapphires and ecotourist attractions might both be understood as "one of a kind" in two ways. First, they are one of a kind in the conventional sense of this expression—that is, in how they offer foreign consumers unique and irreproducible gemstones and touristic encounters that can only be sourced in a location like this. As we zoom out from Ankarana, however, and consider how the economic value of these natural resources is realized through the various processes and transformations that make consumable commodities of them, it becomes clear that they are also one of a kind in another way—that is, in the sense that any one of them is, in fact, one among many of a kind, and thus fairly generic and largely interchangeable. Understanding how Ankarana's sapphires and ecotourist attractions are valued as uniquely *one* of a kind supports the notion that the region has been blessed with plenty; understanding how these same natural resources are made generically one *of a kind* through the workings of the global bazaar, meanwhile, helps to explain why local people seem cursedly unable to benefit more from the "natural" bounty around them.

While understanding how Ankarana's sapphires and ecotourist attractions are valued as one of a kind in two ways can help us to account for the paradox facing people in the region, the complex entanglement of foreign consumers in the knots discussed in the preceding chapters becomes apparent only when we consider how these resources also have something essential in common. In this chapter's final section I discuss how Ankarana's sapphires and ecotourist attractions might also both be considered "natural wonders"—that is, commodities that are valued in large part for a "naturalness" (Ferry 2005:423) that affects, inspires or otherwise arouses wonder in the people attracted to them. If you, like me, have ever felt something when seeing, picking, buying, wearing, giving or receiving a gemstone, a flower or some other natural wonder, you may find that you are more interested than you know in what occupies so many people in Ankarana.

Ankarana's Sapphires from Source to Showcase

As noted at the end of Chapter 2, people in Ambondromifehy often asked me questions that they assumed that I, a foreigner interested in the local sapphire trade, should be able to answer: What are sapphires used for? What happens to them when they leave the region? Why are they so valuable? I admit that these were not questions I had thought much about before spending time in Ambondromifehy. The curiosity of my questioners was contagious, however, leading me to study what I could of the international sapphire trade by reading books and specialty magazines, attending gemmology seminars and trade shows, and consulting marketing material and gemmologists. While places like Ankarana are sources of sapphires, these publications, gatherings, ads, and specialists are sources of something just as important to the global sapphire bazaar: they are the all-important sources of "ponderable news" (Geertz 1979: 203) through which participants outside Madagascar (and some within) must sift in the search for information that is essential to their dealings with one another. Although research based on these sources was quite different from the kind I had done previously in Ambondromifehy, it was no less enlightening. Or humbling. The more I learned about the international sapphire trade, the more I came to appreciate how right Ambondromifehy's miners and traders were in rejecting simple explanations of how it all works. Let me begin with some basics.

Sapphire is the name given to several different colour varieties of a mineral called corundum. Although best known for coming in hues of blue, sapphires can also be yellow, pink, green, and orange; red corundum is better known as ruby. Sapphires tend to be small (most weighing less than one gram) and are very hard (second only to diamonds on the Mohs hardness scale), and thus make for especially portable and durable repositories of the economic value associated with them. Historically, they have been sourced in places all over the world—in Kashmir, Australia, Burma/Myanmar, Ceylon/Sri Lanka, and Thailand, for example—but since the 1990s, an increasing proportion of the global supply of sapphires has been coming out of Madagascar. Not long after Ankarana's sapphires appeared on the global scene in the late 1990s, a gemmological report described Ankarana as "one of the most important sources for cuttable rough sapphire material in the world" (Schwarz, Kanis, and Schmetzer 2000: 216).

I wasn't wrong in suggesting to Ambondromifehy's miners and traders that the stones from which they made their living were destined to be used in the manufacture of jewellery for foreign consumers. In fact, sapphires are among the most highly valued of precious gemstones, with blue sapphires, in particular, regularly appearing atop the best-seller lists of jewellers in Europe, Japan, and North America, where the bulk of them are sold (Zrobowski 2007: 24). But Ambondromifehy's speculators weren't entirely wrong either in imagining that sapphires must have some *other*, more practical, use. In fact, corundum—the material of sapphires—*is* used in some of the practical ways that these speculators imagined: in the manufacture of the windows of military vehicles and artificial hip implants, for example. Such practical uses require large quantities of colourless and perfectly clear corundum, however, and since such sapphire material would never be found in the ground in a place like Ankarana, it must be sourced elsewhere and in a way that neither Ambondromifehy's speculators nor I knew about when we first met.

It turns out that sapphires need not come out of the ground at all—corundum, and thus sapphires, can also be produced in laboratories. While most "synthetic," lab-produced, corundum is made to be colourless and used in the manufacture of durable products like those noted above, it can also be produced in any number of colours and then cut up and transformed into gemstones. As described by Chatham, a company that specializes in the production of what they term "created" gems and gemstone jewellery, the only difference between synthetic sapphires and their "natural" counterparts is that "one [kind] came out of the ground and the other from the laboratory" (Chatham Created Gemstones n.d.; see also Clary 2007). Chemically, optically, and materially, natural and synthetic sapphires are identical, meaning that it takes a trained gemmologist to tell the difference between them. Natural and synthetic sapphires do differ in some ways, however. For example, synthetic sapphires routinely exhibit levels of clarity and a depth of colour that are found in only the rarest natural specimens; since they are produced under controlled conditions, synthetics just about always come out of the lab looking perfect. Indeed, consumers intent on buying natural sapphires are often advised to be wary of stones that look *too* good, as they are likely to be synthetics. Another clear sign of a synthetic sapphire is its asking price. Even synthetic stones that have been produced using the most expensive and time-consuming techniques cost a fraction of the price of natural stones of comparable size, colour, and clarity.

Let me recap: not only are synthetic sapphires materially identical to natural sapphires, but they come in a wide range of colours, tend to be perfect-looking, and cost a fraction the price. Why, then, is there still a market for natural sapphires? More to the point, in a world where synthesizing sapphires in a laboratory is possible, why does a sapphire-mining town like Ambondromifehy even exist? Obviously, there is more to sapphires than meets the eye.

According to the American Gem Trade Association (AGTA), an organization that labels itself the "authoritative source on natural colored gemstones" (AGTA n.d.a), there is no mystery as to what makes natural gemstones so much more valuable than synthetics:

Like flowers, colored gemstones come in every hue, tone and saturation. Both are born of Nature and evolve into something exquisite. But unlike flowers whose beauty fades with time, the beauty of colored gemstones is everlasting. Gathered from all corners of the world every colored gemstone is a unique creation that brings with it a rich history that blends the mystery of Nature with the skill of man. (AGTA n.d.b)

Here, the AGTA compares natural gemstones to flowers in a way that evokes associations with "Nature" that could never stick with synthetics, adopting the two-pronged argument put forward by most natural gemstone dealers I have met over the years: (1) "real" gemstones come out of the ground, and (2) there is simply no substitute for the "real" thing. And consumers would seem to agree. Demand for "natural" coloured gemstones is stronger than ever today, even despite more than a century of competition from synthetic alternatives (Beard 2008).

Since most jewellery consumers can't tell the difference between synthetic and natural sapphires, let alone between natural sapphires that come from one source and those that come from another, they are very much like all players in the global sapphire bazaar in that they rely on others to provide them with the information they need to be sure that they are getting what they want. Thus, for example, anyone buying an expensive piece of jewellery featuring a large natural sapphire is likely to request and receive a certificate, produced by a trained and licensed gemmologist, that attests to the stone's origin. Gemmological testing is time-consuming, expensive, and simply not feasible for most of the natural gemstones sold in the world today, however, meaning that most consumers must look elsewhere for the assurances they need. Retailers understand this need, and while they may not always be able to offer certificates that connect particular stones with particular sources, they are certainly able to represent their own connections with such sources. In *The Gem Merchant: How to Be One, How to Deal with One*, Epstein proposes one way of doing so in his discussion of gemstone "trunk shows" (2003: 85)—events at which an independent gem trader operates through an established jeweller to sell some of his stock. A sure-fire theme for a trunk show, Epstein suggests, is one that stresses connections to gemstone sources. Such a show should be preceded by promotional material alerting customers of a particular jewellery shop to the impending arrival of "The Man Who Romances the Stone"—he "who goes to the deep dark jungles at the four corners of the earth to retrieve eternal beauty which expresses love and devotion in our hearts" (2003:

86)—and should culminate with "The Man" in question appearing at the shop, offering stones, expert advice, and stories to its customers.

Stories of going to the source also appear on the home shopping channels and websites through which a great deal of natural gemstone jewellery is sold today. On the home shopping channel GemsTV, for example, one can watch the channel's hosts on "Gem Adventures" appearing at the actual sources of the merchandise they sell. In one of these adventures, a GemsTV host explores some of the most remote sources of Madagascar's gemstones, leading viewers across hot landscapes and, in a memorable scene, into the depths of a mining pit where, lit by a candle and accompanied by a young Malagasy miner, he makes a compelling case for the great value of all natural gemstones:

> 30 metres underground here in Madagascar, and Radi [*pointing to the miner standing with him*] is one of the local miners, and [he] brings us some beautiful gemstones and we forget this at home … we're sitting in the studio some days and looking at [a gemstone] and this [*pointing again to Radi*] is the sort of gentleman who will bring it out of the ground for us. It's very easy sometimes to look at these elegant gemstones and forget all the hard work that goes into mining them. That's where I see the value. We're looking at so many different gems to bring back to you and Radi does this every day … (Gem Adventures Madagascar n.d.)

Obviously, such depictions of the hard work that goes on at the sources of natural sapphires are not intended to turn consumers off in the manner of journalistic exposés. Quite the opposite, in fact. In the same way that highlighting connections with sources is meant to inspire buyers' confidence in the expertise of dealers and the authenticity of what they offer, highlighting the hard work that goes on at these sources supports the notion that natural gemstones are rare items, hard to procure but worth the premium that consumers will pay for them. There is nothing clean or easy about getting natural sapphires out of the ground, the pitch goes, and they are thus quite unlike the lab-produced alternatives vying for consumers' attention. We mustn't imagine, however, that this public valorization of the work that goes on at natural sapphire sources does anything for the miners who actually do the work. As noted in Chapter 2, the global sapphire bazaar works in such a way that miners are destined to be paid least of all for what they "bring out of the ground." Nor should we let the

Sapphire mining pits near Ambondromifehy.

valorization of sources themselves lead us to imagine that it is only what goes on in places like Ankarana that makes these gemstones so valuable. In fact, it is only *after* natural sapphires leave their sources that they take on the shapes, colours, and other qualities that most consumers expect to find in the gemstones they buy.

As noted in Chapter 2, most of Ankarana's sapphires are destined for Thailand, where they are transformed from rough to finished gemstones. Like all gemstones, most are cut, ground, faceted, and polished into one of several standard shapes that consumers expect them to take: brilliant-cut, marquise-cut, pear-cut, cabochon, etc. Because the characteristic sparkle of a cut sapphire is more the product of the cutter's skill than of the stone's internal properties, cutting must be expertly done, and while Thailand no longer has nearly the supply of natural sapphires that Madagascar does, its long history as a centre of the global sapphire trade has left it with no short-age of skilled and experienced gemstone cutters. While being processed in Thailand, almost all of Ankarana's sapphires undergo various treatments or "enhancements" as well. Like most natural sapphires circulating in the world today, for example, the majority of them are heated at high tempera-tures over extended periods of time in a process that brings out colours and degrees of clarity that are not apparent in them when they have just been taken from the ground. Some also undergo surface-diffusion treatments, which involve coating them with a foreign element such as beryllium and then heating them so as to enable this foreign element's diffusion into the stone through its surface. The effects of surface-diffusion treatments can be dramatic, transforming "very low value rough" sapphires (Emmett 2011: 1) into vibrantly coloured, and highly prized, "fancy" ones (Emmett et al. 2003) that can sell for a great deal. *If* disclosed, such treatments would inevitably lower the value of the sapphires on which they were used. As Omar (the foreign trader discussed in Chapter 2) knew, however, some such treatments can be kept secret for years before the world's gemmologists, retailers, and consumers ever catch on (Hughes 2002).

Just how "natural" are sapphires that change so radically on their way from mine to showcase? Voicing the worry of many observers in the industry, Beesley wonders whether there is "a point at which a material formed within the earth is so processed by man that it can no longer be considered natural" (2008: 38). Such a point may be looming, but it seems not to have come yet. Even when labels like "enhanced," "composite" or "heated with elements" are applied to mined sapphires that have been treated, they seem not to take away from consumers' understandings of the essential naturalness of these stones. As Thompson argues, citing the words of a Toronto jeweller, "customers understand natural to mean a stone that is mined, as opposed to one that is manufactured. While they want a 'real' stone ... for many 'an enhanced one is really enough'" (Thompson 2006: 61). Sales numbers seem to support this perspective. In recent times, as one after another previously unknown treatment has been reported, the volume of the global trade in natural sapphires has only grown (Beard 2008). We should remember, however, that such growth is attributable largely to the fact that what treatments like the ones listed above do most effectively is to supply growing global demand for attractive and low-cost, but still "natural," sapphires. Indeed, the global natural-sapphire bazaar has come to excel at supplying great quantities of finished gemstones that are generic enough to meet the needs of large retailers that sell great quantities of low-cost and attractive, but still "natural," sapphire jewellery. For the Walmarts of the world and their customers, any one pair of $99 natural-sapphire earrings must look exactly like any other.

What becomes very apparent as we follow natural sapphires around the world from their sources in places like Ankarana to their ultimate destinations on the fingers and earlobes of the world's consumers is that any single natural sapphire might be understood as one of a kind in two ways simultaneously. As something that has come out of the ground and then been carefully processed by experienced hands, it is one of a kind in the sense stressed by the American Gem Trade Association: a "unique creation that brings with it a rich history that blends the mystery of Nature with the skill of man" (AGTA n.d.b.). In making its way through the global bazaar, however, such a sapphire is also rendered generically one of a kind—that is, one among thousands of other cut, polished, treated, and set natural sapphires that are destined ultimately to be marketed to, and consumed by, people for whom *any* of their kind will do, so long as it meets a fairly narrow range of aesthetic expectations. Although the sources of natural sapphires do matter in that these locations, and what goes on at them, are guarantees of authenticity, whether the stones come from out of the ground in Ankarana, Thailand, Cambodia, Nigeria, or other sources matters little to most consumers. Indeed, the global sapphire bazaar works in such a way that Ankarana's sapphires might even be radically transformed through treatments and then passed off, by unscrupulous traders, as having come from some *other* source.

This brings me to the last of the questions with which I began this section: What makes Ankarana's sapphires so valuable? Although one of the points made in the preceding pages is that Ankarana's miners and traders stand to benefit the least from the global sapphire bazaar in which they have become involved, it is worth remembering that locally mined and traded sapphires are certainly worth a great deal more to people like Jao, Roby, and Madame Fernand now than they were as the slingshot pellets they once were. No matter how much they might be materially transformed as they make their way around the world, the most important transformations that natural sapphires undergo are transformations in how they are valued (cf. Munn 1986; see also Graeber 2001, Ferry 2005).

Shortly, I will discuss how Ankarana's sapphires might be classified as "natural wonders"—that is, commodities that embody "naturalness" (Ferry 2005: 424) in ways that can affect, inspire or otherwise arouse wonder in the consumers who will pay most for them in the end. Careful readers will note that this is not the first time I have used this phrase—in Chapters 1 and 3, I suggested that the Ankarana massif and its surrounding forests have been considered "natural wonders" to foreign scientists, conservationists, and visitors over the years as well. The call-back is intentional. In fact, considering what it is about Ankarana National Park's natural wonders that draws foreigners to the region can help to broaden our understanding of this category so as to make a simple point that many of Ankarana's speculators correctly assume: what draws foreign visitors to Ankarana

National Park is not so different from what draws them to the sapphires coming out of the region.

The Appeal of Chameleons

Imagine yourself doing a mundane chore in front of your home. A truck pulls up to the side of the road, just a few metres away, and four passengers descend. The one among them who speaks your language explains to you that the other three are visitors interested in the animals that live around you. You point out such an animal crossing the road, sending these visitors into a photographing frenzy; one of them even lies down on the asphalt to get a better shot. Another shows interest in what *you* are doing and takes an incompetent turn at your chore; more pictures are taken. Before they leave, they give you a pen.

This scenario was described to me in 2004 by Eliane, a woman living in Mahamasina, just south of the main entrance to Ankarana National Park. There she stood one day by the side of the road, pounding the husks off of freshly harvested rice, when a group of foreigners and their Malagasy guide pulled up, got out of their truck, and gave her a story to tell. The animal she had pointed out to them—a chameleon—was a familiar sight to her, leading her to ask the same question that I would surely ask if I ever saw

Close-up of a chameleon.

someone lying in the middle of the road outside my home taking pictures of a squirrel: Why would they ever want to do such a thing? Unlike questions I had been asked about sapphires in previous years, Eliane's question about why foreigners are attracted to chameleons was one that past experience had prepared me for. Upon my own first encounter with a chameleon in Ankarana, during the first week of my first visit to the region in 1992, I did exactly what the foreigners Eliane described had done—I lay down on the ground, propped my camera only a few feet away, and took a series of close-ups. I'm not sure why that chameleon fascinated me … it just *did*.

That I struggled to explain the appeal of chameleons to Eliane hints at the complexity inherent in how foreigners value Ankarana's distinctive biodiversity. As our conversation continued, however, it was Eliane who made the most obvious observation. Whatever it was that had brought the foreigners she described to her doorstep, it was certainly worth a great deal more to them than the pen they had given her—she had been hoping that they would give her money in return for pointing out something so valuable. For Eliane, as for other local observers who don't participate in the region's ecotourist trade, no amount of talk about the inherent value of the region's chameleons and other ecotourist attractions changes the simple fact that the local people being asked to conserve such things benefit very little from wealthy foreign visitors who think so highly of them.

The attractions that ecotourists come to see in Ankarana National Park are certainly one of a kind in the conventional sense of this expression—indeed, the fact that they are unique and seemingly irreplaceable is what gives them their must-see appeal. Ankarana's ecotourist attractions are also one of a kind in the second sense introduced earlier, however, in that they are generic and largely interchangeable examples of a *kind* of attraction. To better understand these points, it is worth considering how Madagascar's environments have long been understood by foreigners as one-of-a-kind in these two ways simultaneously.

The first written use of the word "Madagascar" is commonly attributed to Marco Polo, the Venetian merchant whose tales of voyages in the late thirteenth century are among the most celebrated and influential travel accounts in history. Given that Polo had never actually visited what he termed "the Great Island of Madagascar" (Polo 1958), the surprisingly long list of details he offers about the place is understandably short on accuracy—there is nothing right, for example, in his report that Madagascar was home to both elephants and elephant-hunting birds. Still, Polo's account of a rich, fertile, and, ultimately, inviting island full of bizarre wildlife, natural resources, and exotic people eager to exchange with outsiders set a template for the portrayals of several centuries to come. By the nineteenth century, certain species of flora and fauna had begun to take centre stage in many of these accounts. In all cases, however, reports of these *new* discoveries only ever made sense to the foreign explorers, missionaries, scientists, traders, and audiences concerned with them in comparison to *others* of a kind with which they were already familiar (Feeley-Harnik 2001; Anderson n.d.). Indeed, the fact that the island was first described in writing to Europeans by someone who had never actually visited it suggests that even before it was known as "Madagascar," the island was destined to fit on a pre-existing shelf in the European imagination—that is, as one among many distant, distinctive, exotic, and unusual places that author and audiences alike could imagine might well be home to a bird large enough to carry elephants away in its talons.

Today, there is no shortage of sources from which foreigners might draw images of Madagascar as one of a kind. In the last episode of a three-part nature documentary series produced by the BBC, for example, famed naturalist and host David Attenborough makes the standard case for how the island is uniquely one of a kind, noting that "most of Madagascar's wildlife exists nowhere else in the world" (BBC 2011). Over a montage of spectacular footage, some of it depicting crowned lemurs crawling around atop Ankarana's *tsingy*, his narration continues:

> The entire island is a hotspot of biological diversity; a treasure-house of natural riches that is one of the most significant on Earth. Each species has adapted in its own way to the extremes of climate and landscape. But many of them are under threat from loss of habitat, from climate change, from hunting. They are the same perils that face so much of the world's wildlife. But here they are especially poignant. Madagascar is an unrepeatable experiment. A site of unique animals and plants evolving in isolation for over 60 million years. We're still trying to unravel its mysteries. How tragic it would be if we lost it before we even understood it. (BBC 2011)

Not much has changed. Indeed, just 20 years earlier, in an episode of *National Geographic*'s *The World's Last Great Places* (*National Geographic* n.d.) series of documentaries, Madagascar's situation is described with similar awe and pessimism as a place "made rich by the ages" and "alive with natural wonders," but also a "refuge under siege" in which "time is running out." Put yet another way, Madagascar isn't simply one of the world's

Living Edens, as the title of a PBS series featuring an episode on the island suggests; it is a "Paradise in Peril," according to that series' companion website (PBS n.d.). Not that imperilled environments are enough to keep adventurous documentarians and celebrity hosts away, however. Indeed, were the island's lemurs and chameleons *not* endangered, they would never have earned Madagascar a slot in another BBC series called *Last Chance to See: A Search for Animals on the Edge of Extinction* (BBC 2009).

In addition to presenting Madagascar's biodiversity as unique and threatened, nature documentaries like those noted above also put the island on a list of other places of a certain kind—a list that, going by other episode titles of the series mentioned above, includes Namibia's "hostile dunes," Panama's "rainforest of life," India's "Elephant Mountain," and at least four oases of "wilderness." In making this simple point, I don't mean to downplay the distinctiveness of the ecosystems found in each of these places, or to minimize the threats that they currently face. The point, rather, is to note how easy it is for a place like Madagascar to be one of a kind in two ways at once. Had the Madagascar-centric episodes of any of the previously named documentary series not been produced, National Geographic, PBS or the BBC would doubtless have had little trouble filling the missing slot by choosing from another on the growing list of the world's last great Edenic homes to animals on the edge of extinction.

In presenting Madagascar in the way that they do, nature documentaries, magazine profiles, newspaper travel articles, and other popular sources of information about the island do more than just educate foreigners about the country's wildlife—they attract foreigners *to* it as well; following the three-part BBC series cited above, for example, UK-based web inquiries into flights to the island increased substantially (Skyscanner 2011). Not surprisingly, then, many of the most appealing aspects of these documentary portrayals can also be found repeated by the island's own Ministry of Tourism, as well as by foreign travel agencies, tour operators, and others interested in attracting more foreign tourists to Madagascar. Consider, for example, the description of Madagascar offered by the travel agency through which I generally I book my flights to the island. Madagascar, the agency's website declares, is "untouched," "unspoiled," and "undiscovered," an

> Eden-like garden of riches, filled with a diversity of life and geography
> unequaled anywhere else on Earth ... Indeed, every expedition into her
> mountains, her rain forests, her river valleys, her coastal plains, her
> grasslands, her caverns, and her deserts leads to the discovery of some

new plant or animal species. It is no exaggeration to claim that this micro-continent, as some have called it, offers limitless opportunities for exploration. (Cortez Travel 2005)

In such marketing, Madagascar is presented as a one-of-a-kind destination for vacationing explorers intent on new discoveries. Googling "ecotourism" along with some of the keywords and phrases found in this description of the island, however, reveals how it is also a one-of-a-kind destination in the second sense introduced earlier. Madagascar is by no means the only "Eden-like" tourist destination in the world, for example; one online source offers a list of other choices that include Morocco, Dubai, Thailand, and Fiji. Similarly, Latvia's nature has been described as "untouched," Taiwan's environments are "undiscovered," Tobago is "unspoiled," and plentiful "opportunities for exploration" can be found in Argentina, Finland, Uganda, Vancouver Island, and the Amazon rainforest. Obviously, the fact that ecotourist destinations as diverse as these are presented to consumers in many of the same ways has less to do with what such places have in common than it does with what is shared by the people who are targeted by such marketing. But what makes ecotourists such good targets for such images? Why is it that the sort of people who stopped in front of Eliane's house are drawn to "Eden-like," "untouched," "undiscovered," and "unspoiled" places that offer "opportunities for exploration"?

In an influential study of the phenomenon of modern tourism, MacCannell argues that tourist attractions offer researchers nothing less than "direct access" to the "world views" of the people they attract (1999: 2). In recent years, several researchers have considered ecotourist attractions and destinations with this insight in mind. Summarizing some of this research, Duffy highlights how ecotourists are commonly "thought to be sensitive travelers who seek to reduce the impacts of their holiday-making" (2002: 22), for example, and are "generally defined as" having "an interest in outdoor pursuits" and as being "financially comfortable, well-educated, older people with free time to travel" (23, citing work by Ballantine and Eagles). They are also, as MacCannell's *Tourist* was, concerned with discovering novelty and authenticity in the places they visit. Indeed, as Duffy notes, "[t]his search for novelty and an 'authentic' pre-industrial nature" (2002: 24) is what distinguishes ecotourists from more conventional, "mass," tourists from whom they often wish to distinguish themselves.

In a different source, Duffy discusses Madagascar specifically, noting how promoters of the promise of ecotourism on the island often use the "terms of neo-liberalism" to argue "[that] the country has a 'comparative advantage' in nature, adventure and cultural tours." According to such thinking, Duffy continues,

> Madagascar has a unique environment, and in terms of recognition as a "brand" in the global tourism market, it has the great benefit of the highly charismatic and instantly recognizable lemurs. ... In fact, the Malagasy environment and wildlife tourism "product" has no equivalent competition because endemic lemurs cannot be viewed anywhere else. (Duffy 2006: 134)

Madagascar's "brand" as a one-of-a-kind destination in the global ecotourist industry, in other words, is seemingly unassailable. And yet, as Duffy's work suggests, the fact that Madagascar is understood by ecotourism promoters as having a "brand" at all indicates quite clearly that, whatever its "comparative advantage," it must compete with other options in an increasingly crowded marketplace.

It would be a mistake to see ecotourism as an outcome of nothing but the desires and motivations of the consumers who undertake it, however. Ecotourism is also a business that, like any other, thrives or falters depending on how well it meets the expectations of the consumers it serves. And although such consumers may arrive in places like Madagascar intent on discovering the novelties promised by guidebooks and tour operators, such new discoveries tend to proceed in familiar ways. As West and Carrier (2004) argue, enabling ecotourists to access what is distinctive about ecotourist destinations often requires that local environments be reshaped and local lives recast in ways that conform to fairly generic "Western idealizations" of nature and society (2004: 485).

In Ankarana National Park, ecotourists' expectations have been addressed by blazing the hiking trails that will lead them from one new discovery to another, by building elevated viewing platforms from which they can gaze upon, and photograph, postcard vistas of the apparently unspoiled and Edenic wilderness being explored, and, most recently, by constructing a rope bridge on which adventurous hikers can wobble over the park's famed *tsingy*. Much in the way that treating, cutting, and polishing renders a rough sapphire from Ankarana into the sparkling gemstone that foreign consumers expect it to be, what the paths, platforms, and rope bridges that one finds in Ankarana and other ecotourist destinations do is to enable consumers to find what they expect in what attracts them. And what exactly *does* attract them? When you ask ecotourists visiting Ankarana why they have come to the place, their first answers are the ones you'd expect: they come to see the attractions for which the region has become so well known. Paying close attention to the stories they tell about the time they spend in the region, however, the complexity of their encounters with this one-of-a-kind place becomes clearer. Consider, for example, the case of Joan, a 60-year-old Australian ecotourist with whom I toured Ankarana National Park over several days in 2004.

By the time Joan arrived in Ankarana, she was on the last leg of a two-month bicycle tour that had taken her around the country along roads leading from one of Madagascar's National Parks to another. Madagascar was only one in a long list of places (including India, Vietnam, and Ghana) she had visited since retiring from a career in environmental management. Her interest in these destinations stemmed not simply from her long-standing fascination with the distinctive sorts of what she called "intact" ecosytems that can be found in them, but also, she explained, from a "long-lived interest in people ... [in] rural communities [and how] they live their lives in the environment [and] use whatever is in the environment for their livelihood." This latter interest was itself a product of her dissatisfaction with what she knew from her experience of wasteful "Western culture." Not surprisingly, urban environments held no interest for Joan on trips like this, except as necessary stops where she could find a bank, a good meal, and a shower. Nor was she interested in what she termed the "artificial" experiences on offer at beach resort areas elsewhere in Madagascar. "[Tourists] who go there have no feeling of connection to the land they're in, the landscape, or the people who live there," she noted. "They're there for a good time, they go for a fishing trip, or they sit in the bar to pick up girls. You could do that anywhere ... it becomes ... a hedonistic respite from [their] normal life."

While I would never call Joan a typical ecotourist—Robert taught me that there is no such thing—her story suggests a range of interests and concerns that researchers have identified as being common to the type: an interest in environments unlike those to be found at home (and a corresponding concern that they remain "original"); an interest in local people who live in harmony with such environments (and a concern with the destructive tendencies of those who do not); and an interest in unspoiled traditional cultures (and a concern for the harm being caused by what she termed "modernization" and foreign influences). For Joan, the experience of the travel that enabled her to pursue these interests was clearly as important as the places she visited. Indeed, as noted above, she was like many of the visitors to Ankarana that I have met over the years in identifying herself and her travel habits in opposition to other forms of tourism that she considered environmentally and socially irresponsible. She was intent on distinctive experiences that would be rewarding to her as well as to the local people with whom she shared them.

Where does all of this leave us in our efforts at understanding the appeal of chameleons to the tourists who stopped in front of Eliane's house? However unusual and memorable these foreigners were to Eliane, it should be clear by now that they were far from exceptional. In fact, they exhibited textbook ecotourist behaviour, taking an interest in, and photos of, Madagascar's distinctive wildlife and people; as one recent survey of visitors to Malagasy National Parks indicates, chameleons are, after lemurs, "the second most important animal group for ecotourists visiting Madagascar" (Wollenberg et al. 2011: 115). With that in mind, one way of understanding the encounter that Eliane shared with these visitors is as precisely the kind of encounter these visitors were seeking in Madagascar. In fact, what may have surprised Eliane most is what she didn't see but I am certain must exist: namely, the hundreds of photographs that these foreigners had taken of similar encounters at *other* stops on their trip—maybe even pictures of *other* chameleons and *other* puzzled Malagasy observers standing at the roadside. Although it seems unlikely that these photos would ever be sold, as Eliane had thought might be the case, they were valuable nonetheless, providing those who took them with a record of a one-of-a-kind encounter in a one-of-a-kind place that would almost certainly end up in an album filled with photos of other encounters and places of much the same kind.

Natural Wonders

Although understanding how Ankarana's sapphires and ecotourist attractions are one of a kind in two ways can help us to understand the paradox with which I began this chapter, this approach comes with a paradox of its own: If foreign consumers find Ankarana's sapphires and ecotourist attractions so appealing because they are one of a kind in the first way—that is, in the sense of being unique and irreproducible—how do they manage to consume them as such knowing that they are also one of a kind in the second way, i.e., as fairly generic and largely interchangeable with others of their kind? How is it, in other words, that gemstone jewellery consumers and ecotourists can consume the generic as unique? It would be a mistake to dismiss this paradox by portraying foreign consumers as the unwitting dupes of a global bazaar in which more knowledgeable others tell and sell them only what they want to know and buy. However clever the marketing of jewellers and travel agencies might be, and however oblivious consumers might wish to remain, advertising and indifference only go so far in helping us understand the *source* of foreign consumers' fascination with natural sapphires and ecotourist attractions.

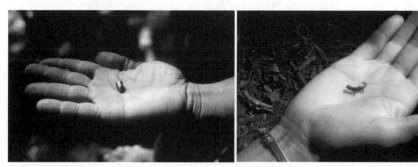

Left: A sapphire in the palm of the miner who brought it out of Ankarana National Park. Right: A Brookesia chameleon from Madagascar, among the world's smallest reptiles.

In this chapter's final section, I argue that the unique, one-of-a-kind quality that foreign consumers associate with Ankarana's sapphires and ecotourist attractions is remarkably resistant to the corrosive possibilities of knowing or realizing that these same sapphires and ecotourist attractions are also among many of a kind. More precisely, I suggest that Ankarana's sapphires and ecotourist attractions might be understood as natural wonders—commodities that manage to be both unquestionably unique and acceptably generic in appearing to have certain inherent, affective qualities that no amount of polish or packaging could ever take away from them. Although this apparently inherent one-of-a-kindness certainly has its material manifestations—of the sort that might be certified by gemmologists or protected by conservationists—it presents itself most obviously not in what natural sapphires and ecotourist attractions *are*, but in what they can *do* to consumers. To make sense of what I mean by this, it helps to return to Ambondromifehy.

Eric was one of the traders who questioned me about the uses of sapphires in the years before I began the research discussed in this chapter. During a visit to Ambondromifehy in 2006, I had the chance to answer him. I began by telling him that the material of sapphires *is* sometimes put to use in the practical ways that he and other speculators had imagined, but that such uses require perfectly clear and colourless *synthetic* corundum of the sort that is produced in a laboratory; sapphires coming out of the ground around Ambondromifehy, I noted, are destined for making jewellery. I went on to stress what I found most puzzling about all this: gem-quality synthetic sapphires look perfect and cost a fraction of what comparable stones from Ankarana would, yet many foreign consumers still prefer natural sapphires. Were it not for this last fact, I suggested, the town in which we were sitting and talking would not exist. Eric was not as perplexed by all of this as I had expected he might be. In fact, by discussing the existence of synthetic alternatives to locally mined sapphires, I had clarified things for him. By his estimation, foreigners who prefer and are willing to pay more for sapphires that come out of the ground rightly value what he termed "the work of God"—*asan'ny zagnahary*—over human-made alternatives.

The phrase "the work of God" is one that Malagasy people I have known over the years use in several different ways. Most commonly, it is used with reference to events or things that catch you off guard or amaze you, or both: events and things, in other words, that are obviously not the work of people and over which people have no control—everything from unexpected deaths, to cyclones, to unusually shaped tree trunks. It is also an expression that was used several times by guides and conservation workers in Mahamasina to explain what attracts foreigner visitors to Ankarana National Park. Anne, the park employee mentioned in the previous chapter, for example, suggested that foreigners come to Ankarana because it is one of the few places left in the world in which they can experience the sort of "authentic" (a term that she related in French) nature that is no longer available to them in the places they come from. What these foreigners can't get at zoos and botanical gardens in Europe and North America, others suggested, is the experience of wandering through and wondering at an environment that they haven't made for themselves—an environment that is, as several suggested, the "work of God."

While I am reluctant to argue, as Eric and others might, that the capacity of Ankarana's sapphires and ecotourist attractions to attract consumers is a reflection of the "work of God" in our world, it is certainly more than just the work of jewellers and travel agents. In making sense of what I found so puzzling, Eric recognized the simple point that natural sapphires appeal to foreign consumers not simply because they were *made* to do so. Rather, they appeal to them because they are so easily imagined to have been made—or, more accurately, to have come into being—quite apart from the human social processes, desires, and trends that have made commodities of them. The same might be said of Ankarana's ecotourist attractions; the chameleon I photographed in 1992 didn't fascinate me because it was designed (in the way an iPad is) by people who knew what kind of thing I might find fascinating ... it just *did*. In one sense, this seemingly inherent "naturalness" (Ferry 2005: 424) is as undeniable as the geological and biological processes that have made sapphires and chameleons available in Ankarana; indeed, it is such processes that make every one of the region's sapphires and chameleons uniquely one of a kind in its own way. In another sense, however, the naturalness of these natural wonders is potentially compromised by the social processes involved in their commodification (Ferry 2005)—the mining, cutting, and selling that make Ankarana's natural sapphires much like any other of their kind, for example, or the boundary maintenance, trail making, and touring that have put Ankarana's natural areas on the must-see lists of so many of the world's travellers. And while opinion may differ on how much and what sorts of human interventions threaten the naturalness of Ankarana's sapphires and ecotourist attractions—Is a heat-treated sapphire "natural"? Is a paved road inside the reserve "*naturel*"?—to those who perceive naturalness in these natural wonders there is little question over what distinguishes them from their clearly *un*natural alternatives.

I imagine that few readers found it surprising to learn that gemstone traders often refer to natural sapphires as "real" in order to distinguish them from synthetic stones. Nor, I imagine, were many surprised at the disparaging tone in Joan's comments about the "artificial" experiences on offer at Madagascar's beach resorts. For many of us, "authenticity" is an especially valuable quality to be celebrated in what is "real," "true" or "genuine," while "inauthenticity" is something more likely to be exposed in what is "artificial," "false" or "fake." Celebrating authenticity as a feature of consumable things (like sapphires) or experiences (like travel) is a relatively recent phenomenon, however. As Lindholm (2008) argues, it has only been over the past century, as many of the world's wealthiest consumers have begun seeking and carving out distinctive identities for themselves through what they buy, that consuming "the real thing" has come to matter as much as it does today. The argument, simply put, is that over this period, as consumers have become disillusioned with the mass-production and marketing of commodities through which they might distinguish themselves from others, the "[c]onsumption of various forms of commodified authenticity" has provided "anxious buyers with feelings of autonomy, control, community, as well as feelings of distinction, status, and self-actualization" (2008: 56).

The authenticity that consumers associate with natural sapphires is of a sort shared by other one-of-a-kind commodities that are valued as much for how they came to be as for what they are—commodities such as artwork, handicrafts, archaeological artifacts, or hand-woven carpets, for example. An important feature of such things is that although they can be, and often are, copied, the distinctive origins that make them authentic can never be reproduced. Thus, while a carpet produced on a mechanical loom in a Chinese factory might look a lot like one made on a hand-operated loom in a Turkish village, to many consumers there is no doubt as to which is the more authentic and thus the more valuable (Spooner 1986). In fact, rather than threaten the market for what is being copied, near facsimiles such as factory-made carpets or synthetic sapphires can highlight the authenticity of what is deemed authentic, opening the possibility for important distinctions to be drawn not just among "real" things and their copies, but also among the people who value, pursue, and choose to buy one or the other. The similarities between natural sapphires and other things valued for their distinctive origins only go so far, however, in that what makes natural sapphires authentic has little to do with the work that people put into them. Indeed, what makes natural sapphires authentic is that they are understood to have originated *without* human intention or intervention. And this is a quality they share with Ankarana's ecotourist attractions.

As Anne noted, Ankarana's ecotourist attractions might also be considered sites at which a form of commodified authenticity is consumed. Indeed, in bringing up the idea that visitors are searching for something "*authentique*" in Ankarana National Park, Anne put herself alongside MacCannell, Duffy, West and Carrier, and a long list of other observers who have noted tourists' desire for encounters with the authentic in their travels. In discussing the touristic pursuit of authenticity, Lindholm focuses especially on consumers who look to explore and discover social and natural environments unlike those they can find at home—people like Joan (the ecotourist introduced in the previous chapter) who want to go off the beaten path trodden by conventional tourists. The most authentic of these experiences, as some see it, are likely to come unexpectedly, and the least authentic among them are those that must be paid for. So, when you happen upon a woman pounding rice by the side of the road and share an encounter with her unlike any you'd have in an artificial beach resort nearby, better to leave her with the gift of a pen than a payment of money, lest you cheapen the experience for both of you.

Within Ankarana National Park, it is relatively easy to consume "commodified authenticity" apart from "the corrosion of commercialism" (Lindholm 2008: 43) that ecotourists like Joan clearly shun. Although ecotourists' experiences inside the park are certainly enabled by a great number of commercial transactions—with travel agents, tour operators, and guides, for example—the authenticity on offer here is easily imagined to be well distinct from such transactions. If anything, the money paid to discover this place—park fees in particular—can appear to guarantee the authenticity that ecotourists seek here, given that, as promoters of ecotourism promise, it would seem to offer local people an economic incentive for embracing conservation.

It is not only the "naturalness" or "authenticity" of Ankarana's natural wonders that makes them one of a kind, however. In fact, they are most powerfully realized as uniquely one of a kind not in what they *are* but in what they can *do* to people—in how a sapphire mined in Madagascar can elicit the passionate reaction of a gem-lover "drawn into" its "silken world" (Hughes 2001; see this chapter's epigraph), for example, or how Ankarana's spectacular landscape can rouse the "Wowwwww!" of a visitor gazing over it for the first time. As commodities that affect, inspire or otherwise arouse wonder in those who are drawn to them, we might understand Ankarana's natural wonders as having a capacity akin to those of "fetishes"—that is, the capacity to "'naturally' embody socially significant values that touch one or more individuals in an intensely personal way" (Pietz 1985: 13–14). What makes fetishes special is that their capacity to "touch" (or awe, or dazzle, or wow, or fascinate) appears to the people they *do* touch as being inherent or, as Pietz puts it, "natural"—a capacity that is "of" them rather than some-thing that people give to them (Pels 1998). In the case at hand, the affective and "socially significant" value that Ankarana's natural wonders seem to "naturally" embody is naturalness itself. And, judging by the reactions it arouses in those who value it most, this naturalness is priceless—not in the sense that consumers will pay any amount for the experience of it, but that the value it gives things is "absolute" and incomparable rather than "relative" and economically rationalized (Lambek 2008: 135). Insofar as this natural-ness touches those who are attracted to it in "intensely personal" ways, the natural wonders of which this quality is an essential part are destined to be appreciated as uniquely one of a kind, no matter how many others of their kind there might be. Although any appealing natural sapphire might arouse passion in a gem lover, and any ecotourist attraction viewed from a rope-bridge might elicit a "wow!," this doesn't lessen their one-of-a-kind impact on the consumers they affect at any given moment.

It is a strange thing to over-think what foreign consumers find so appealing about Ankarana's natural wonders. While concepts like those introduced in the preceding pages can certainly help us make sense of the characteristic quality that these natural wonders share, the quality in question may, in fact, be better understood as something that people *feel* than something they, or we, might conceptualize. Indeed, as a quality that is felt—experienced emotionally and subjectively—the quality I have in mind is something that many won't need a grounding in anthropological concepts to appreciate. If you have ever been drawn to a brightly coloured flower, been intrigued by the patterning of a smooth rock on a beach, or been captivated by a sunset over a still lake, you know the feeling I am getting at here. If you have ever picked that flower (or picked up something like it in a garden centre), pocketed that stone (or bought an even more intriguing one at a museum gift shop), or pitched a tent at the side of that lake (or thought of building a deck there on which you might barbeque), then you know the tempting possibilities for extraction and consumption that can come with being affected by such things. If you have ever gifted a flower to a loved one, waxed nostalgic over a childhood rock collection, or shared a sunset with a friend, then you know how social the natural can be. And, finally, if you have ever been disappointed to learn that the flower that drew you in from a distance was revealed up close to be plastic, that the stone's smoothness was a product of a rock-tumbler rather than waves, or that the apparent beauty of the sunset in front of you is a result of smog, then you know full well the complexity of the calculations that go into determining the value of natural wonders.

How much the feelings aroused by natural wonders are products of the distinctive backgrounds and histories of those who experience them, and how much comes from what all humans share as one-of-a-kind members of a single species is a matter for debate. For the purposes of this book, it is enough to know that such feelings are by no means unfamiliar to many of the people with whom I've been working in Madagascar. They are certainly familiar to a shopkeeper in Ambondromifehy who took cuttings from plants he found inside Ankarana National Park so that he might grow them in plastic buckets in front of his home, for example, as well as to the Malagasy graduate student whose Facebook album of "wonderful moments" from a recent visit to Canada contains no less than four pictures of squirrels. This shouldn't be surprising. As noted in the previous two chapters, the fact that people in Madagascar are interested in many of the same things as foreign consumers was never in question to people in Ankarana. After all, what makes us different from one another is not only to be found in how we attribute affective capacities to things like stones and trees differently, but in our own differential capacities to access and control these things. By now, it should not surprise you to learn that in taking a plant cutting out of Ankarana National Park the shopkeeper mentioned above broke the law, or that it is far more difficult for a Malagasy graduate student to get close to a Canadian squirrel than for a Canadian graduate student to get close to one of Ankarana's chameleons.

However influential Ankarana's natural wonders have been in firing the imaginations of the foreigners whose demand has made commodities of them, they have been even more influential in how they have shaped the reality of people discussed in the previous three chapters. Simply put: Were Ankarana's natural sapphires and ecotourist attractions *not* valued by foreigners in the way that they are, neither Ambondromifehy nor Mahamasina would look anything like they do now. Jao, the "daring" miner described in Chapter 2, would probably still be working at the port in Antsiranana; Robert, the guide described in Chapter 3, might be driving a bush taxi. We must be careful, however, not to take this state of affairs as a sign that the twenty-first-century global economy works in the very simple way that advocates of the promise of neoliberal capitalism imagine—that is, as a means for funnelling the wealth of the world's richest consumers directly into the hands of people like Jao and Robert, who are in a position to supply their demands. As I hope is obvious by now, such clear and mutually beneficial connections are never so easily realized in the global bazaar.

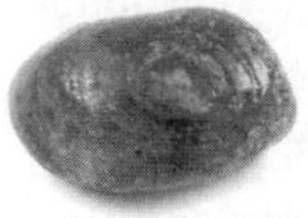

CONCLUSION: SO WHAT?

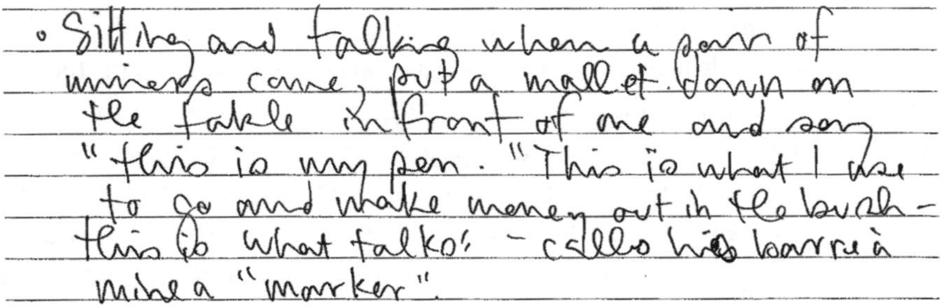
• Sitting and talking when a pair of miners came, put a mallet down on the table in front of me and say "this is my pen." "This is what I use to go and make money out in the bush—this is what talks" —calls his barre à mine a "marker".

A field-note written in Ambondromifehy.

I am sitting and talking with traders in a booth on Ambondromifehy's strip—pen and notebook in hand—when a pair of miners comes by. One puts his mining hammer (used to break up clumps of earth in his pit) down on the counter in front of me and says: "This is *my* pen—this is what I use to make money out in the bush. This is what talks." He calls the "mining bar" he uses "a marker."

A more legible version of the above.

This book was made in Madagascar. It originated in thousands of encounters like the one recounted, twice, above—encounters that were often first documented through mad scribbling in a notebook, and then processed into something more informative, and legible, on a computer. As promised in Chapter 1, I have used my stock of such encounters to produce discussions of topics and phenomena that might have been studied just about anywhere in the world. The final product, however, could have come from no other source.

This book was also made outside of Madagascar. It has been typed up in Canada and France, in offices and coffee-shops, on desktops and laptops, informed by consultations with colleagues and their work, and enriched by insights drawn from the unlikeliest sources—from seeing a woman pick up, fold, and pocket two petals of a purple magnolia blossom, for example; from hours spent watching a home-shopping channel; and from my daughters' rock and pine-cone collections. Readers who are new to anthropology might want to take this as a warning: as I have learned to do it, anthropology is an especially engrossing vocation in which the line between the study of social life and the living of it can get fuzzy (Lambek 2005).

Most recently, it is a table at Starbucks that has caught my attention—the small round table in the corner, near the electrical outlet, at which I have occasionally been working on what you've just read. Here, printed around the circumference of this table's top, are four lines of text that capture a revealing vision of the global bazaar. Although the text runs in a circle, there is no question as to where it begins: "*i grow the beans*," the first line states, alongside a stylized figure carrying a coffee plant on its head; "*so what!*," says the next figure in the cycle, "*i roast them*"; "*but i give them flavor*," says a third, leading us, finally, to a barista and the last word: "*i give them brewability*." It would be hard to imagine a simpler depiction of the politics of value-added in the global economy today—18 words and one callous exclamation point that effectively illustrate how what goes on at the sources of something that the world's wealthiest consumers can't live without is simultaneously valued and *de*valued. You may already have guessed at the line that says most to me: "*so what!*" So ... what?

To conclude, I address this last question in two different ways. First, I offer one more look at the global bazaar, illustrating as I close how the simultaneous valuing and devaluing of sources that come with Starbucks' vision of the world is more than just an academic problem. Second, I discuss the speculating that people in Ankarana have done about my research and me over the years, and consider what these speculations might tell us about the dilemmas and value inherent in doing anthropology today.

Ankarana in the Global Bazaar

Even though you've read what you've just read, you may still not care all that much about Ankarana's sapphires—you might think that a synthetic one is just as good, for example, or that all gemstones might just as well be slingshot pellets. You may also have no desire to visit an ecotourist attraction in Ankarana—you might prefer to stay home or to embrace the comforts of a beach resort. Maybe Ankarana's sapphires and ecotourist attractions just don't strike you as all that wonderful; or maybe they are out of your price range. If any or all of this is true, how might you relate to the global bazaar I have tried to describe in this book?

Chances are that the coffee you drank this morning comes originally from somewhere far away, and that what brought it to you was the global bazaar; the same goes for tea-drinkers. Don't drink coffee or tea? Is there paint on the walls of the room you are in? There is a good chance that the base pigment of this paint is made of ilmenite, another mineral that comes out of the ground in Madagascar. Are your walls unpainted? Do you have a cell phone, then? The battery that powers your cell phone is made of, among other things, "rare earth" minerals that are also found in Madagascar. You get the idea. If you aren't *already* a player in the global bazaar glimpsed in this book, you are living on another planet.

Although you may believe, as Starbucks marketing suggests, that "geography is a flavour," and while you may value the gentle spiciness offered by Guatemalan coffee beans or the earthy aroma of those from Sumatra, the pleasure you take in coffee would not be so rich, flavourful, or convenient without everything that goes on once these beans leave their sources; nor would the jolt it gives you be so cheap without the undervalued work that goes on in such places. Not that all of this is likely to concern you too much. In fact, you may not think about all the work that goes into producing a cup of coffee any more than you think about what goes into a can of paint or about what makes your cell phone work. These commodities do what you need them to do, and any questions you have about them probably stem from immediate concerns: Single or double espresso? What colour of paint? Is it too soon for an upgrade? As you sip your coffee, you may even be headed for, or deep into, work of your own. Obviously, this is precisely what I was doing when I first encountered the tabletop cited above.

The global systems and processes that I saw at work in and from Ankarana are the same ones that bring the world's coffee beans to Starbucks and other coffee shops; they are also what bring ilmenite out of Madagascar and draw foreign "rare earth" prospectors to the island. But you didn't need me to tell you that. Learning how we are all already involved, or how we might involve ourselves differently, in the global bazaar has never been easier. If you thought googling "Madagascar" produced a lot of links, you should try googling "coffee." Better yet, you might try directing an Internet search at learning how coffee, like Ankarana's sapphires and ecotourist destinations, is a commodity that is one of a kind in two ways—something that provides coffee drinkers with something unique while providing coffee growers with the uncertain opportunities of producing something generic. You might also consider doing similar searches on "ilmenite" or "rare earths." What you are likely to find in such searches, however, is that, as in any bazaar economy, having *more* "ponderable news" at your disposal doesn't always clarify things; as Geertz wrote, "coming to decisions about what to make of" all of the information circulating in the noisy networks of a bazaar economy is no easy task, and "[k]eeping your feet in the bazaar mob is mainly a matter of deciding whom, what, and how much to believe" (Geertz 1979: 203). And so you, like people in Ankarana, may be inclined to simply learn what you can and keep going.

This book was never intended to be a buyer's guide. It was written, rather, in order to offer a distinctive perspective on the global systems and processes that shape so much of our world. In Ankarana—in the wake of sapphires and among the hosts and guides of foreign ecotourists—the political and economic forces that affect everyone in the world couldn't be more apparent. Indeed, as I have stressed many times, the lives of people in Ambondromifehy and Mahamasina would not be what they were if not for their involvement in the global bazaar; in a world without jewellery buyers and adventurous travellers, Jao might still be daring and Robert might still be walking through the forest, but not in the ways described in Chapters 2 and 3. What I have described in this book has also come, however, from recognizing one of the great ironies that the global bazaar has brought to Ankarana. If we zoom out from either Ambondromifehy or Mahamasina, far enough to take in the other location as well as the National Park alongside which both communities have developed, we can see how the region's sapphire and ecotourist trades have made unlikely opponents of their participants—rendering Jao's mining a threat to Robert's livelihood as a guide, for example, and putting Robert's desire to conserve what he considers valuable in Ankarana National Park in opposition to Jao's desire to extract the same thing. Some might be tempted to see conflicts of interest like these as nothing but glitches in the otherwise humming global systems and processes that make things like natural sapphires and places like Ankarana National Park the valuable commodities they have become. As I have presented the sources and consequences of this glitch here, however, I hope you will consider it otherwise.

Zooming out from Madagascar, we see quite clearly what people in Ankarana can only speculate about—namely, how it is that, as described in Chapter 4, people in this region are systematically marginalized in a global economy that provides foreign consumers with gemstones and touristic experiences that are *both* unique, irreplaceable, and absolutely valuable, *and* generic, interchangeable, and thus relatively cheap. As I have described it, the global bazaar is a buyer's market that presents a world of choices to foreign consumers and a world of paradoxes and limited possibilities to people in places like Ankarana. And I hope that my description of it might inspire you to go on speculating. To me, the fact that Ankarana's natural wonders so often affect those who are drawn to them in the way that they do only sharpens the paradox facing people in the region: how is it that those who provide and conserve what brings nothing less than *wonderment* to so many in the world can benefit so little from doing so?

There is no denying that Ankarana's sapphire and ecotourist trades have benefitted people in Ankarana to some extent. Indeed, I have *no* doubt as to the answer you would get if you asked Jao if you ought to buy one of the region's sapphires, or Robert if you ought to visit one of its ecotourist attractions. Unfortunately, conversations that might connect you directly with people in Ankarana are very difficult to manage in the global bazaar, so those who benefit the most from your interest in what the region has to offer are those who make its natural wonders accessible, and "legible" (Scott 1999, West and Carrier 2004), to you. There may be ways of forging and mediating clearer connections in the international sapphire and ecotourist trades (see, for example, Cartier and Pardieu 2012, Stronza 2001), but they are rarely as convenient as their alternatives. And even with clearer connections, the systemic problems facing people in a position to serve global demand for natural wonders are hard to shake. Recent events have only confirmed this point.

In 2008, the Malagasy government enforced unprecedented restrictions on the export of rough gemstones from Madagascar in an effort to exert greater control over an industry that had clearly done more to benefit foreigners than Malagasy people. Many foreign gemstone traders responded by simply leaving the island, and with their departure, Ambondromifehy's traders suddenly had far fewer buyers for the stones in which they had invested a great deal. As you might expect, some foreign traders left owing money to the Malagasy traders with whom they had built up trusting relationships over the years, promising to return once the crisis had ended. As of my last visit in 2010, only a few of them had returned. Omar was back in Thailand; Gan, a Thai buyer with whom I had often spoken in Ambondromifehy in previous years, was in Tanzania trading in another blue gemstone called tanzanite.

Late in 2008, a gemstone rush close to another nearby protected area emptied Ambondromifehy of miners and traders intent on a return to "the life!" and to the opportunities that sapphires had once brought them. The gemstone they were looking for—demantoid, a kind of green garnet—was rumoured to be plentiful and valuable, but it wasn't easy to get at. I never got to the site of this new rush, but you won't be surprised to learn that an online retailer of specimens sourced there offers prospective customers both photos and a vivid description of what it was like. "800 INDIVIDUAL mining holes" had been dug in a mangrove swamp:

> 800 holes requires 800 teams of diggers, haulers, and sorters; and so you can imagine the crowd during working hours of some 2000-2500 people in this swamp, all flowing in and out with the tides of water. To reach the garnet layer, the miners have to dig straight down (literally, in vertical, rope "hanging seats"), 10-20 meters below the surface. When they hit garnet-bearing rock, they then branch sideways, each miner's group making their own tunnels where they wish and without apparent regard for the gradually honeycombing structure of the rock caused by other mining teams above, beside, and below them. (Arkenstone Fine Minerals n.d.)

And while miners were risking and daring in their work, traders were doing the same—trying to apply lessons learned from sapphires to this latest discovery. In the end, though, most of those who had left Ambondromifehy returned after a few months, several of them worse off for their time away. Hoping to score big, as the first sapphire buyers in Ambondromifehy had in the late 1990s, several traders I spoke with in 2010 had made the mistake of buying up too much, too soon, and for too high a price without any certainty of finding foreign buyers.

Things were just as uncertain for many I visited in Mahamasina in 2010. In 2009, the ruling Malagasy government was ousted amidst popular outrage over corruption and reports of a deal to lease huge expanses of Malagasy land to a Korean agribusiness venture. The violence and instability that came with this coup was reported around the world, and many foreign governments warned their citizens against travelling to Madagascar. The impact on Ankarana's ecotourist trade was profound. After years of increasing

Demantoid (green garnet) mined in a new rush to the south of Ambondromifehy in 2009.

popularity, Ankarana National Park saw a 50-per-cent drop in visitors in one year, and with this dip, the livelihoods of Mahamasina's guides were jeopardized and the ecotourism-related projects of local entrepreneurs and community organizations were put on hold, if not destroyed entirely (Colquhoun, Totomarovario, and Walsh 2011; see also Hunter 2011 and Patterson 2011).

The events of 2008 and 2009 were crises to people who had come to depend on Ankarana's sapphire and ecotourist trades. They were nothing of the sort, however, to the foreign consumers whose demand had made these trades viable in the first place—both natural sapphires and ecotourist attractions can be found in any number of places around the world, and whatever opportunities for the consumption of luxuries, authenticity, adventure, naturalness or wonderment were lost as a result of the events just described were by no means irreplaceable. Anyone interested in Madagascar's sapphires and ecotourist attractions need look no further than Tanzania, just across the Mozambique Channel, where precious blue gemstones and rare chameleons can also be found side by side.

Obviously, the big issues addressed in this book are bigger than any single study, or even a single discipline, could hope to address. Thankfully, anyone interested in learning more about the past and present social, political, and economic systems and processes that have given rise to the global bazaar has no shortage of sources to consider. Many of these sources will help you make better sense of how we have come to live in a world in which saying "*so what!*" to coffee growers helps Starbucks sell more coffee, or how depictions of the awful uncertainties of mining can help to sell gemstones (Wolf 1982, Mintz 1985, and Harvey 2005, for example). Others will help to better situate the push for nature conservation in the midst of a changing global economy (Brockington, Duffy, and Igoe 2008). Still others will offer more on how people have come to value commodities such as coffee, sapphires, and ecotourist attractions, as well as ideas such as authenticity and naturalness, in the way that they do (Appadurai 1986, Graeber 2001, and Lambek 2008, for example). As you search outside of Ankarana, however, I would encourage you not to lose sight of other places with which this region has much in common—the coffee-producing highlands of Papua New Guinea (West 2012), for example, or the diamond fields of Angola (De Boeck 2001), or Tanzania's coastal vacation spots (Walley 2004), to name just three. As seen from the perspectives of people living in these places, the workings of the global bazaar are consequential, paradoxical, obvious, constraining, liberating, and thought-provoking in ways that reveal not just the callousness, but also the shortsightedness, of saying "*so what!*" to them.

Since anthropological research often leads its practitioners to spend years concentrating on topics that some people can't imagine being all that important, we anthropologists are used to hearing variations of "*so what!*" in response to our work. We are also used to being asked "so what?" by funding agencies, colleagues in other disciplines, policy makers, students, and, of course, the people with whom we spend hours sitting, talking, and learning as we go about our research. *You* may find your work interesting, they say, but of what use is it to *us*? In the most inspiring responses to such questioning, anthropologists have taken on new commitments and collaborations, within academia and beyond, in ways that make the most of what our discipline has to offer those outside of it (see, for example, Field and Fox 2007, Eriksen 2006, Lassiter 2005). It is more difficult, however, to address the dissatisfaction of those who consider an anthropological perspective to be irrelevant, counter-productive or subversive because it can't crank out the easy solutions or short answers that some seek in it. But the fact that anthropology can't provide easy solutions to obvious problems, or simple answers to short questions, is not a flaw of the discipline. In fact, anthropology is often *most* productive in exposing the lie that easy solutions or simple answers might exist. And in this respect, anthropology is bound to disappoint some. To me, however, and to the kindred researchers, teachers, and students with whom I have worked over the years, the fact that anthropology only ever complicates the world we think we know is what most recommends it.

I conclude this book where it began—with its sources. Given the questions and speculations discussed in Chapters 2 and 3—questions about the uses to which foreigners put sapphires, for example, and speculations about the *real* interests of foreigners visiting Ankarana National Park—it won't surprise you to learn that the people from whom I learned so much of what I've presented in these pages had questions and speculations about *me* and about what I was doing in their midst. How is it, people would sometimes ask, that someone like me can earn money from what I do? How do I manage to transform notebooks full of messy scribbles into a livelihood that not only keeps me alive but enables me to come back to Ankarana year after year after year? In one conversation, a trader in Ambondromifehy pointed out what was surely obvious to many: the fact that, like foreign sapphire traders and foreign visitors to Ankarana National Park, I would not have travelled halfway around the world, leaving my comfortable Canadian home for this uncomfortable Malagasy mining town, if I wasn't in pursuit of something valuable. The book or articles I would write would be sold, he surmised, and my efforts would pay off handsomely in the end. The scribbled notes I was gathering day in and day out were *my* sapphires— they were things that "are small [i.e., insignificant] here ... [but that] will become big [i.e., valuable] overseas." Such a comparison between my work and the work of the sapphire trade was even more forcefully made in the encounter described in the epigraph to this Conclusion. "This is *my* pen," said the miner, putting his hammer down in front of my open notebook, "This is what I use to make money out in the bush."

In the early years of the research that went into this book, I answered questions and speculations like these with stories of the uncertainties of trying to find research funding in Canada, of academic journals that require authors to pay fees to have their work considered for publication, and of the difficulties of finding a job in anthropology. As for the book I would write ... this one has taken me more than ten years to finish, and what little money it generates in the form of author's royalties will go into a fund dedicated to supporting the research and travel of Malagasy university students. As time went on, however, and I was lucky enough to find funding and jobs that would allow me to keep coming back to Ankarana, there was no denying the obvious. The research behind this book *has* been the product of a great many privileges. To clarify what I mean by this, I will return to Ambondromifehy one last time.

One morning in 2004, I recorded a conversation with a group of sapphire miners and traders. The topic was a familiar one: foreigners and what makes them different from Malagasy people. Bera, a trader, spoke first. As he saw it, what makes the foreigners who come to Ankarana so different from the Malagasy people who live here is their "way of looking at things." Bera noted that

> When foreigners look at something, ... they look at it deeply. They ask themselves whether [a] thing is true or not. Does it have any meaning, or no meaning? Only when they've done this do they leave it.

Later in the conversation, Bera continued along these lines, explaining how looking at things "deeply" in the way he had in mind is both something that foreigners learn to do and something they are *able* to do. He illustrated his point with the hypothetical example of a Malagasy child who wants to learn how to fix watches. He explained that no Malagasy parent could afford to give his or her child a watch to practice or tinker with, knowing that there is a good chance that the child might break it. For wealthier foreigners, however, what is another watch? Getting back to his main point, Bera speculated that the children of foreigners are *encouraged* to engage in prospective play—that is, they are encouraged to dismantle watches and other things, to play with and look at them deeply, to examine their inner workings in order to get at and understand what makes them tick. Fixing the watch is not the point; it is the prospective play itself that is important, ensuring unknowable future benefits to those who can afford to engage in it now. Bera then linked his example to the situation in Ankarana. Who knows why foreigners visit Ankarana National Park, whether they are conservationists, tourists, explorers, prospectors, or something else? What was obvious was that even if it might seem like they are only playing here, foreigners' interest in this place is telling in and of itself. Foreigners in Ankarana never just look; they are always looking for a reason.

At my instigation, the conversation eventually turned from the prospective play of foreigners to the possible uses that foreigners might have for sapphires. Having had enough, a miner named François announced his leave by slinging his mining bar across his shoulder and remarking that he didn't care what foreigners did with sapphires, as long as they kept buying them; it was time for him to leave my workplace and get back to his own. I remember François well because, up to the moment he left, his contribution to the conversation was composed almost entirely of questions. "I want to ask you something," he always began, "Are there crazy people where you are from?" or "Are there Malagasy people where you are from?" or "How long does it take to get here from where you are from?" Others in our group urged him not to take us off the topics I had proposed, but I assured them all, and François in particular, that I was always happy for opportunities to share what I know with people who had always been so generous in doing the same. And so as the conversation proceeded, I answered François's questions as best I could. Before he walked away, I thanked him for taking part in the conversation. He thanked me in return. "This has been a good talk that we have had here," he said,

> ... we have spoken about many things. When I think back on it, there will be some things that I will take and apply in my daily life. The things that I don't like, I have heard them but I won't use them. It is like what you do. The things that are significant to you, you will write down in your book. The things that aren't [important to you] get taken away by the wind.

As François understood perfectly well, my interest in the conversation we shared was essentially prospective. He rightly assumed that I would not use all of his and others' recorded words—I would sift through them, picking out the passages most significant to me, and then write them down in my book; and he was right too that in trying to make his words, and other encounters, legible to others, much would be left aside or "taken away by the wind." Although it was true that I spoke Malagasy better than any foreign traders and that I didn't spend time in Ankarana National Park like foreign tourists did, these peculiarities didn't make my prospective approach any less obvious. It was there in my digital recorder, and in the fact that I asked questions in Malagasy but scribbled answers in English. It was there in my asking different people the same questions over and over again, in my stories of travel to and from Madagascar, and in my promises to return again in the near future.

The sort of prospective play that Bera attributed to foreigners, and that François observed in my habits, is not an approach taken by all foreigners in or toward Madagascar; I have certainly met many over the years who have no interest in deeply considering the complexities of the place. Nor is it only foreigners who engage in such prospective play; many Malagasy biologists, historians, and other researchers do the same. There was, however, something distinctive about the *anthropological* research that had led me into this conversation with Bera, François, and others. As MacClancy notes, what often distinguishes anthropologists' efforts at addressing the complexities they are studying is that they have learned to "listen to ... competing voices of members from different interest groups ... [and to] compare their words with their deeds in order to disentangle the overlapping realities, and ... clarify ... various misconceptions and consequent confusions" (2002b: 421). Often, we consider as much as we can in preparing to write what we do because we can never be sure what will and will not be important from the start. The same uncertainty prevails when contemplating the end results of our work. "The boundaries of what is 'socially relevant' research," MacClancy writes, "are constantly shifting, in tune with changing circumstances. What may appear to be abstruse scholarship one day may become material of great political import the next day" (2002a: 14). This *prospective* outlook is one that I have learned to take in my work, and one that I share with many others in the discipline. It is also, of course, precisely the perspective that François, Bera, and others in Ankarana might expect of a relatively privileged prospective player like me. Although they are uncertain and often ask about how I am able to make a living from doing what I do, they understand perfectly well that I am able to take the prospective view that I so obviously do because I *can*.

Over the past century, anthropological research methods and priorities have developed within the same powerful global systems that have influenced Ankarana's development. Critiques and commentaries from observers of anthropologists over this period offer important reminders of this simple fact (see, for example, Asad 1995, Biolsi and Zimmerman 1997, and Tehindrazanarivelo 1997), while academic histories of anthropology (see, for example, Kuper 1983, Darnell 2001) consider the complicated and situated commitments of the discipline's practitioners. No amount of mulling over anthropology's development and current practice can offer an easy way out of the dilemmas that come with trying to study human worlds from within their own unequal workings, however. There is something to be said, though, for how anthropological research requires that we take such dilemmas seriously. Although anthropologists are not the only researchers of humanity to enjoy the privilege of prospective play, we tend to see this privilege for what it is more clearly from within the social exchanges that so often engage us in our work than we might if poring over statistics or seated behind a one-way mirror. And this, again, is not a flaw but a great asset of the discipline.

Bera once told me that what made me different from other foreigners he had met in the region is that I "talk to everybody." "What is different [about you]," he said, "is the conversation ... you don't choose among people [to talk with]." In response, I reminded him of what he already knew about me and my work—that is, that these apparently admirable habits of mine are essential to what I do; I "talk to everybody," or at least to as many people as I can, because doing so helps me do a better job of trying to make sense of things in the way that I have learned to. He countered by stressing that this point didn't matter as much as the fact that the two of us were actually having the conversation we were having. As he saw it, whatever else it might be about, my research was valuable for how it required me to speak with, and listen to, *him*—a Malagasy sapphire trader with a distinctive perspective on the world. I can think of no better way of ending what will, for me, always be a work in progress. While there is certainly much to be said for how anthropology enables us, as promised in the Introduction, to study existing links in an interconnected world, the greatest attribute of the discipline may be that it requires us to continually forge *new* links—links that lead to improbable conversations in unlikely settings, to unexpected insights from overlooked sources, and to the prospect of better understandings of a world of often troubling disconnects.

REFERENCES

ADAPT. 1999. *Etude d'Impact Environnemental Approfondie des Activités d'Exploitation du Saphir dans et autour du Parc National de l'Ankarana*. Rapport final.

American Gem Trade Association (AGTA). N.d.a. "AGTA History." http://www.agta.org/about/index.html.

American Gem Trade Association (AGTA). N.d.b. "Gemstone Information." http://www.agta.org/gemstones/index.html.

Anderson, Andrew, David Andrew, Becca Blond, and Tom Parkinson. 2008. *Lonely Planet Madagascar & Comoros*. Oakland, CA: Lonely Planet.

Anderson, Thomas. N.d. "Solving Madagascar: Science, Illustrations, and the Normalizing of Fauna of Nineteenth Century Madagascar." Forthcoming in *The Politics of Marketing Land: Value, Conservation and Development in Madagascar*, ed. Gwyn Campbell, Sandra Evers and Michael Lambek. Leiden: Brill.

Appadurai, Arjun. 1986. "Introduction: Commodities and the Politics of Value." In *The Social Life of Things: Commodities in Cultural Perspective*, ed. Arjun Appadurai, 3–63. Cambridge: Cambridge University Press.

Arkenstone Fine Minerals. N.d. "Garnet—New Finds from Madagascar: A New Locality for Gem Demantoid Garnet!" http://www.irocks.com/Demantoid_Garnet_Topazolite_Garnet_Madagascar_Garnet.html.

Aronica, Ronald, and Mtetwa Ramdoo. 2006. *The World Is Flat?: A Critical Analysis of Thomas L. Friedman's New York Times Bestseller*. Tampa, FL: Meghan-Keffer Press.

Asad, Talal, ed. 1995. *Anthropology and the Colonial Encounter*. Amherst, NY: Prometheus Books.

Astuti, Rita. 1995. *People of the Sea: Identity and Descent among the Vezo of Madagascar*. Cambridge: Cambridge University Press. http://dx.doi.org/10.1017/CBO9780511521041

Bandy, Joe. 1996. "Managing the Other of Nature: Sustainability, Spectacle, and Global Regimes of Capital in Ecotourism." *Public Culture* 8 (3): 539–66. http://dx.doi.org/10.1215/08992363-8-3-539.

Barndt, Deborah. 2002. *Tangled Routes: Women, Work, and Globalization on the Tomato Trail*. Toronto: Garamond Press.

Batchelor, Rev. R.T., and Rev. Bishop Kestell-Cornish. 1877. Notes on the Antankarana and their Country. Antananarivo Annual 3.

BBC. 2009. *Last Chance to See: Aye-aye*. http://www.bbc.co.uk/programmes/boomzxkr

BBC. 2011. *Madagascar: Land of Heat and Dust*. http://www.bbc.co.uk/programmes/b00z03pl

Beard, Morgan. 2008. "Global Gem Explosion." *Colored Stone* 21 (1): 44–47.

Beesley, C.R. 2008. "The Transformers: A Gem Alchemy Timeline." *Colored Stone* 21 (1): 36–39.

Bellows, Keith. 2001. "Madagascar Tourism." http://news.nationalgeographic.com/news/2001/07/0724_TvTravMad.html.

Berger, Laurent. 2012. *Anthropologie de la mondialisation—l'exemple de Madagascar*. Paris: CNRS.

Biolsi, Thomas, and Larry Zimmerman. 1997. *Indians and Anthropologists: Vine Deloria, Jr., and the Critique of Anthropology*. Tucson: University of Arizona Press.

Bloch, Maurice. 1986. *From Blessing to Violence: History and Ideology in the Circumcision Ritual of the Merina*. Cambridge: Cambridge University Press. http://dx.doi.org/10.1017/CBO9780511621673

Bloch, Maurice. 1999. "'Eating' Young Men among the Zafimaniry." In *Ancestors, Power and History in Madagascar*, ed. Karen Middleton, 175–217. Leiden: Brill.

Brockington, Dan. 2002. *Fortress Conservation: The Preservation of the Mkomazi Game Reserve*. Bloomington: Indiana University Press.

Brockington, Dan, Rosaleen Duffy, and Jim Igoe. 2008. *Nature Unbound: Conservation, Capitalism and the Future of Protected Areas*. New York: Routledge.

Cardiff, Scott, and Julien Befourouack. 2003. "The Réserve Spéciale d'Ankarana." In *The Natural History of Madagascar*, ed. S.M. Goodman and J.P. Benstead, 1501–7. Chicago: University of Chicago Press.

Cardiff, Scott G., Fanja H. Ratrimomanarivo, Guillaume Rembert, and Steven M. Goodman. 2009. "Hunting, Disturbance and Roost Persistence of Bats in Caves at Ankarana, Northern Madagascar." *African Journal of Ecology* 47 (4): 640–9. http://dx.doi.org/10.1111/j.1365-2028.2008.01015.x.

Cartier, Laurent E., and Vincent Pardieu. 2012. "Conservation Gemstones: Beyond Fair Trade?" National Geographic News Watch. http://newswatch.nationalgeographic.com/2012/01/12/conservation-gemstones-beyond-fair-trade/.

Cerwonka, Allaine, and Liisa H. Malkki. 2007. *Improvising Theory: Process and Temporality in Ethnographic Fieldwork*. Chicago: University of Chicago Press.

Chatham Created Gemstones. N.d. http://www.chatham.com

CIA World Factbook. 2012 . "Madagascar." https://www.cia.gov/library/publications/the-world-factbook/geos/ma.html.

Clary, Leslie Jordan. 2007. "Synthetics City." *Colored Stone* 20 (1): 34–37.

Colquhoun, Ian, Alex Totomarovario, and Andrew Walsh. 2011. "Good Neighbors." *Anthropology News* 52 (3): 7.

Conklin, Beth A., and Laura R. Graham. 1995. "The Shifting Middle Ground: Amazonian Indians and Eco-Politics." *American Anthropologist* 97 (4): 695–710. http://dx.doi.org/10.1525/aa.1995.97.4.02a00120.

Conservation International. N.d. The biodiversity hotspots. http://www.conservation.org/where/priority_areas/hotspots/Pages/hotspots_main.aspx.

Cortez Travel. 2005. "Madagascar. Untouched. Unspoiled. Undiscovered." http://www.air-mad.com/.

Darnell, Regna. 2001. *Invisible Genealogies: A History of Americanist Anthropology*. Lincoln: University of Nebraska Press.

Day, Sophie, Evthymios Papataxiarchis, and Michael Stewart, eds. 1999. *Lilies of the Field: Marginal People Who Live for the Moment*. Boulder, CO: Westview Press.

De Boeck, Filip. 2001. "Garimpeiro Worlds: Digging, Dying & 'Hunting' for Diamonds in Angola." Review of *African Political Economy* 28 (90): 548–62.

Dolan, Catherine S. 2007. "Market Affections: Moral Encounters with Kenyan Fairtrade Flowers." *Ethnos* 72 (2): 239–61. http://dx.doi.org/10.1080/00141840701396573.

Duffy, Rosaleen. 2002. *A Trip Too Far: Ecotourism, Politics and Exploitation.* London: Earthscan Publications.

Duffy, Rosaleen. 2006. "Global Environmental Governance and the Politics of Ecotourism in Madagascar." *Journal of Ecotourism* 5 (1–2): 128–44. http://dx.doi.org/10.1080/14724040608668451.

Duffy, Rosaleen. 2007. "Gemstone Mining in Madagascar: Transnational Networks, Criminalization, and Global Integration." *Journal of Modern African Studies* 45 (2): 185–206. http://dx.doi.org/10.1017/S0022278X07002509.

Duffy, Rosaleen. 2010. *Nature Crime: How We're Getting Conservation Wrong.* New Haven, CT: Yale University Press.

Durbin, Joanna C., and Solo-Nirina Ratrimoarisaona. 1996. "Can Tourism Make a Major Contribution to the Conservation of Protected Areas in Madagascar?" *Biodiversity and Conservation* 5 (3): 345–53. http://dx.doi.org/10.1007/BF00051778.

Eggert, Karl. 1986. "Mahafaly as Misnomer." In *Madagascar: Society and History*, ed. Conrad Kottak, Jean-Aime Rakotoarisoa, and Aidan Southal, 321–35. Durham, NC: Carolina Academic Press.

Emmett, John L. 2011. "Of Beryllium and Beefsteak." *The GemGuide* (Jan./Feb.): 1–9.

Emmett, John L., Kenneth Scarratt, Shane F. McClure, Thomas Moses, Troy R. Douthit, Richard Hughes, Steven Novak, James E. Shigley, Wuyi Wang, Owen Bordelon, et al. 2003. "Beryllium Diffusion of Ruby and Sapphire." *Gems and Gemology* 39 (2): 84–135. http://dx.doi.org/10.5741/GEMS.39.2.84.

Epstein, D.S. 2003. *The Gem Merchant: How to Be One, How to Deal with One.* Piermont, NY: Gem Market.

Eriksen, Thomas Hylland. 2006. *Engaging Anthropology: The Case for a Public Presence.* Oxford: Berg.

Esoavelomandroso, Manassé. 1989. "Une arme de domination: le 'tribalisme' à Madagascar." In *Les ethnies ont une histoire*, ed. J.-P. Chrétien and G. Prunier, 259–66. Paris: Karthala.

L'Express de Madagascar. 2012. "Plus de 50 000 touristes ont visité Madagascar durant le premier trimestre de 2012, indique le ministre du Tourisme." 28 March 2012. http://lexpressmada.com/2-breves/279-plus_de_50_000_touristes_ont_visite_madagascar_durant_le_premier_trimestre_de_2012_indique_le_ministre_du_tourisme.html.

Feeley-Harnik, Gillian. 2001. "*Ravenala Madagascariensis* Sonnerat: The Historical Ecology of a 'Flagship Species' in Madagascar." *Ethnohistory (Columbus, Ohio)* 48 (1–2): 31–86. http://dx.doi.org/10.1215/00141801-48-1-2-31. Medline:17600968

Ferguson, James. 2006. *Global Shadows: Africa in the Neoliberal World Order.* Durham, NC: Duke University Press.

Ferraro, Paul J. 2002. "The Local Costs of Establishing Protected Areas in Low-income Nations: Ranomafana National Park, Madagascar." *Ecological Economics* 43 (2–3): 261–75. http://dx.doi.org/10.1016/S0921-8009(02)00219-7.

Ferry, Elizabeth Emma. 2005. "Geologies of Power: Value Transformations of Mineral Specimens from Guanajuato, Mexico." *American Ethnologist* 32 (3): 420–36. http://dx.doi.org/10.1525/ae.2005.32.3.420.

Field, Les, and Richard Fox. 2007. *Anthropology Put to Work.* Oxford: Berg.

Fischer, Edward F., and Peter Benson. 2006. *Broccoli and Desire: Global Connections and Maya Struggles in Postwar Guatemala.* Stanford, CA: Stanford University Press.

Freedman, Jim. 1983. "Will the Sheik Use His Blinding Fireball? The Ideology of Professional Wrestling." In *The Celebration of Society: Perspectives on Cultural Performance*, ed. Frank E. Manning, 67–79. Bowling Green, OH: Bowling Green University Popular Press.

Freudenberger, Karen. 2010. *Paradise Lost? Lessons from 25 Years of USAID Environment Programs in Madagascar.* Washington, DC: International Resources Group.

Friedman, Thomas. 2005. *The World is Flat: A Brief History of the Twenty-First Century.* New York: Farrar, Strauss and Giroux.

Geertz, Clifford. 1979. "Suq: The Bazaar Economy in Sefrou." In *Meaning and Order in Moroccan Society: Three Essays in Cultural Analysis*, 123–244. Cambridge: Cambridge University Press.

Gem Adventures Madagascar. N.d. http://www.youtube.com/watch?v=fG6fRXicK-Q&feature=BFa&list=PL58BFE145B5886C2B

Gezon, Lisa. 1997. "Political Ecology and Conflict in Ankarana, Madagascar." *Ethnology* 36 (2): 85–100. http://dx.doi.org/10.2307/3774077.

Gezon, Lisa. 2006. *Global Visions, Local Landscapes: A Political Ecology of Conservation, Conflict, and Control in Northern Madagascar.* Walnut Creek, CA: AltaMira Press.

Giguère, Hélène. 2006 *Des morts des vivants et des choses: Ethnographie d'un village de pêcheurs au nord de Madagascar.* Québec: Les Presses de L'Université Laval.

Graeber, David. 2001. *Towards an Anthropological Theory of Value: The False Coin of Our Own Dreams.* New York: Palgrave Press.

Hanson, Paul. 2007. "Governmentality, Language Ideology, and the Production of Needs in Malagasy Conservation and Development." *Cultural Anthropology* 22 (2): 244–84. http://dx.doi.org/10.1525/can.2007.22.2.244.

Harper, Janice. 2002. *Endangered Species: Health, Illness and Death among Madagascar's People of the Forest.* Durham, NC: Carolina Academic Press.

Harvey, David. 2005. *A Brief History of Neoliberalism.* Oxford: Oxford University Press.

Hughes, Richard. 2001 "Passion Fruit: A Lover's Guide to Sapphire." *The Guide* 20(2): 3–5, 15.

Hughes, Richard. 2002. "The Skin Game." *The Guide* 21 (2): 3–7.

Hunter, Emma. 2011. "Awkward Encounters: Improvisation, Negotiation and Exchange at a Sacred Cave-tomb/Tourist Attraction in Northern Madagascar." MA Thesis, Department of Anthropology, University of Western Ontario.

Igoe, James. 2004. *Conservation and Globalisation: a Study of National Parks and Indigenous Communities from East Africa to South Dakota.* Case Studies in Contemporary Social Issues. Belmont, CA: Wadsworth/Thomson Learning.

Investment Fiji. N.d. "Welcome to Fiji." http://www.investmentfiji.org.fj/.

IPA (Investment Promotion Authority, Papua New Guinea). N.d. "Why Invest in Papua New Guinea." http://www.ipa.gov.pg/index.php?option=com_content&task=view&id=448&Itemid=0.

Jaovelo-Dzao, Robert. 1996. *Mythes, Rites et Transes à Madagascar: Angano, Joro et Tromba Sakalava.* Paris: Karthala.

Jensen, Oystein. 2009. "The Activation of Local Service Suppliers by Incoming Tour Operators in a "Developing" Destination—the Case of Madagascar." *Current Issues in Tourism* 12 (2): 133–63. http://dx.doi.org/10.1080/13683500802549689.

Karl, Terry Lynn. 1997. *The Paradox of Plenty: Oil Booms and Petro-States.* Berkeley: University of California Press.

Kaufmann, Jeffrey C. 2006. "The Sad Opaqueness of the Environmental Crisis in Madagascar." *Conservation & Society* 4 (2): 179–93.

Keller, Eva. 2008. "The Banana Plant and the Moon: Conservation and the Malagasy Ethos of Life in Masoala, Madagascar." *American Ethnologist* 35 (4): 650–64. http://dx.doi.org/10.1111/j.1548-1425.2008.00103.x.

Keller, Eva. 2009. "The Danger of Misunderstanding 'Culture.'" *Madagascar Conservation and Development* 4 (2): 82–85.

Krüger, Oliver. 2005. "The Role of Ecotourism in Conservation: Panacea or Pandora's Box?" *Biodiversity and Conservation* 14 (3): 579–600. http://dx.doi.org/10.1007/s10531-004-3917-4.

Kuper, Adam. 1983. *Anthropology and Anthropologists: The Modern British School*. London: Routledge and Kegan Paul.

Lambek, Michael. 2005. "Afterword: Our Subjects/Ourselves: A View from the Back Seat." In *Auto-Ethnographies: The Anthropology of Academic Practices*, 229–42, ed. Anne Meneley and Donna Young. Toronto: University of Toronto Press.

Lambek, Michael. 2008. "Value and Virtue." *Anthropological Theory* 8 (2): 133–57. http://dx.doi.org/10.1177/1463499608090788.

Lanting, Frans. 1990. *Madagascar: A World out of Time*. New York: Aperture.

Lassiter, Luke Eric. 2005. *The Chicago Guide to Collaborative Ethnography*. Chicago: University of Chicago Press.

Lindholm, Charles. 2008. *Culture and Authenticity*. Oxford: Blackwell.

Lonely Planet. 2012. "Introducing Madagascar." http://www.lonelyplanet.com/madagascar.

MacCannell, Dean. 1999. *The Tourist: A New Theory of the Leisure Class*. Berkeley: University of California Press.

MacClancy, Jeremy. 2002a. "Introduction: Taking People Seriously." In *Exotic No More: Anthropology on the Front Lines*, ed. Jeremy MacClancy, 1–14. Chicago: University of Chicago Press.

MacClancy, Jeremy. 2002b. "Paradise Postponed: The Predicaments of Tourism." In *Exotic No More: Anthropology on the Front Lines*, ed. Jeremy MacClancy, 418–29. Chicago: University of Chicago Press.

Mack, John. 1986. *Madagascar: Island of the Ancestors*. London: British Museum Press.

Madagascar National Parks. N.d. Ankarana. http://www.parcs-madagascar.com/fiche-aire-protegee_en.php?Ap=6#.

Marcus, Richard R. 2001. "Seeing the Forest for the Trees: Integrated Conservation and Development Projects and Local Perceptions of Conservation in Madagascar." *Human Ecology* 29 (4): 381–97. http://dx.doi.org/10.1023/A:1013189720278.

Maurer, David. 1974. *The American Confidence Man*. Springfield, IL: Charles C. Thomas.

Mauss, Marcel. 1990. *The Gift: The Form and Reason for Exchange in Archaic Societies*, trans. W.D. Halls. New York: W.W. Norton.

Middleton, Karen, ed. 1999. *Ancestors, Power and History in Madagascar*. Leiden: Brill.

Mintz, Sidney. 1985. *Sweetness and Power: The Place of Sugar in Modern History*. New York: Viking.

Mulligan, Philip. 1999. "The Marginalization of Indigenous Peoples from Tribal Lands in Southeast Madagascar." *Journal of International Development* 11 (4): 649–59. http://dx.doi.org/10.1002/(SICI)1099-1328(199906)11:4<649::AID-JID605>3.0.CO;2-8.

Munn, Nancy. 1986. *The Fame of Gawa: A Symbolic Study of Value Transformation in a Massim (Papua New Guinea) Society*. Durham, NC: Duke University Press.

National Geographic. 2002. "Sapphire Mining, Madagascar, 1998." Photo of the day (4 Feb. 2002). http://photography.nationalgeographic.com/photography/photo-of-the-day/sapphire-mining.html.

National Geographic. N.d. *Africa: Wilds of Madagascar. World's Last Great Places.* http://shop.nationalgeographic.com/ngs/product/dvds/animals-and-nature/animals-and-wildlife/world's-last-great-places-dvd-set.

Nomadic Thoughts. N.d. "Madagascar." http://www.nomadicthoughts.com/zW/africa/432/madagascar.aspx.

Patterson, Ashley. 2011. "Off the Beaten Path: Obstacles to Success in a Locally Managed Community-based Conservation and Ecotourism Project in Northern Madagascar." MA Thesis, Department of Anthropology, University of Western Ontario.

PBS. N.d. "Madagascar: A World Apart." The Living Edens. http://www.pbs.org/edens/madagascar/.

Pels, Peter. 1998. "The Spirit of Matter: On Fetish, Rarity, Fact and Fancy." In *Border Fetishisms: Material Objects in Unstable Spaces*, ed. Patricia Spyer, 91–121. New York: Routledge.

Peypoch, Nicolas, Rado Randriamboarison, Fy Rasoamananjara, and Bernardin Solonandrasana. 2012. "The Length of Stay of Tourists in Madagascar." *Tourism Management* 33 (5): 1230–5. http://dx.doi.org/10.1016/j.tourman.2011.11.003.

Pietz, William. 1985. "The Problem of the Fetish, I" *Res* 9: 5–17.

Pollini, Jacques. 2011. "The Difficult Reconciliation of Conservation and Development Objectives: The Case of the Malagasy Environmental Action Plan." *Human Organization* 70 (1): 74–87.

Polo, Marco. 1958. *The Travels of Marco Polo*, trans. Ronald Latham. London: Penguin Classics.

Radcliffe-Brown, A.R. 1952. "The Mother's Brother in South Africa." In *Structure and Function in Primitive Society*, 15–31. London: Routledge & Kegan Paul.

Rappaport, Roy. 1979. "The Obvious Aspects of Ritual." In *Ecology, Meaning and Religion*, 174–222. Richmond, CA: North Atlantic Books.

Ross, Michael L. 1999. "The Political Economy of the Resource Curse." *World Politics* 51 (02): 297–322. http://dx.doi.org/10.1017/S0043887100008200.

Sauphanor, chef du district d'Ambilobe. 1939. Monographie du District d'Ambilobe. Archives Nationales d'Outre Mer. Generique: Mad, fonds: DS, cote: ds179.

Sawyer, Suzana. 2004. *Crude Chronicles: Indigenous Politics, Multinational Oil, and Neoliberalism in Ecuador*. Durham, NC: Duke University Press.

Scheffel, Richard L., and Susan J. Wernert, eds. 1980. *Natural Wonders of the World*. New York: The Reader's Digest Association, Inc.

Schwarz, Dietmar, Jan Kanis, and Karl Schmetzer. 2000. "Sapphires from Antsiranana Province, Northern Madagascar." *Gems and Gemology* 36 (3): 216–33. http://dx.doi.org/10.5741/GEMS.36.3.216.

Scott, James. 1999. *Seeing Like a State: How Certain Schemes to Improve the Human Condition Have Failed*. New Haven, CT: Yale University Press.

Skyscanner. 2011. "Estonia, Madagascar and Iraq Emerging Summer Hotspots for Brits, Reveals Skyscanner." *Enhanced Online News*, 25 July 2011. http://eon.businesswire.com/news/eon/20110725005623/en/.

Sodikoff, Genese. 2009. "The Low-Wage Conservationist: Biodiversity and Perversities of Value in Madagascar." *American Anthropologist* 111 (4): 443–55. http://dx.doi.org/10.1111/j.1548-1433.2009.01154.x.

Spooner, Brian. 1986. "Weavers and Dealers: The Authenticity of an Oriental Carpet." In *The Social Life of Things: Commodities in Cultural Perspective*, ed. Arjun Appadurai, 195–235. Cambridge: Cambridge University Press.

Stratton, Arthur. 1965. *The Great Red Island: A Biography of Madagascar*. New York: Macmillan and Co. Ltd.

Stronza, Amanda. 2001. "Anthropology of Tourism: Forging New Ground for Ecotourism and Other Alternatives." *Annual Review of Anthropology* 30 (1): 261–83. http://dx.doi.org/10.1146/annurev.anthro.30.1.261.

Theodore, Jean. 1987. "Le rôle du culte de possession tromba dans le rituel de l'érection du mât en pays antankarana." *Omaly sy Anio* 25-26:41–7.

Tehindrazanarivelo, Emmanuel. 1997. "Fieldwork: The Dance of Power." *Anthropology and Humanism* 22 (1): 54–60. http://dx.doi.org/10.1525/ahu.1997.22.1.54.

Thomas, Philip. 1998. "Conspicuous Construction: Houses, Consumption and 'Relocalization' in Manambondro, Southeast Madagascar." *Journal of the Royal Anthropological Institute* 4 (3): 425–46. http://dx.doi.org/10.2307/3034155.

Thompson, Sharon Elaine. 2006. "It's a Natural." *Canadian Jeweller* (Nov.): 60–61.

Travel and Leisure. 2011. "Explore the Global Bazaar." http://www.travelandleisure.com/promo/globalbazaar/.

Tsing, Anna. 2000. "The Global Situation." *Cultural Anthropology* 15 (3): 327–60. http://dx.doi.org/10.1525/can.2000.15.3.327.

Tsing, Anna. 2005. *Friction: An Ethnography of Global Connection*. Princeton, NJ: Princeton University Press.

Tsitindry, Jeanne-Baptistine. 1987. "Navian'ny Tsangan-tsainy." *Omaly Sy Anio* 25–26: 31–40.

Tyson, Peter. 2000. *The Eighth Continent: Life, Death and Discovery in the Lost World of Madagascar*. New York: William Morrow.

UNICEF. 2012. "Madagascar. Statistics." http://www.unicef.org/infobycountry/madagascar_statistics.html.

Veblen, Thorstein. 1993. *A Veblen Treasury: From Leisure Class to War, Peace and Capitalism*. Armonk, NY: M.E. Sharpe.

Vial, Maurice. 1954. "La Royauté Antankarana." *Bulletin de l'Académie Malgache* 92: 3–26.

Vivanco, Luis A. 2007. *Green Encounters: Shaping and Contesting Environmentalism in Rural Costa Rica*. Oxford: Berghan Books.

Waast, Roland. 1973. *Les Antankarana*. Paris: ORSTOM.

Walley, Christine. 2004. *Rough Waters: Nature and Development in an African Marine Park*. Princeton, NJ: Princeton University Press.

Walsh, Andrew. 2001a. "What Makes (the) Antankarana, Antankarana? Reckoning Group Identity in Northern Madagascar." *Ethnos* 66 (1): 27–48. http://dx.doi.org/10.1080/0014184020042616.

Walsh, Andrew. 2001b. "When Origins Matter: The Politics of Commemoration in Northern Madagascar." *Ethnohistory (Columbus, Ohio)* 48 (1–2): 237–56. http://dx.doi.org/10.1215/00141801-48-1-2-237.

Walsh, Andrew. 2002a. "Preserving Bodies, Saving Souls: Religious Incongruity in a Northern Malagasy Mining Town." *Journal of Religion in Africa. Religion en Afrique* 32 (3): 366–92. http://dx.doi.org/10.1163/157006602760599953.

Walsh, Andrew. 2002b. "Responsibility, Taboos and 'The Freedom to do Otherwise' in Ankarana, Northern Madagascar." *Journal of the Royal Anthropological Institute* 8 (3): 451–68. http://dx.doi.org/10.1111/1467-9655.00117.

Walsh, Andrew. 2003. "'Hot Money' and Daring Consumption in a Northern Malagasy Sapphire-Mining Town." *American Ethnologist* 30 (2): 290–305. http://dx.doi.org/10.1525/ae.2003.30.2.290.

Walsh, Andrew. 2004. "In the Wake of Things: Speculating in and about Sapphires in Northern Madagascar." *American Anthropologist* 106 (2): 225–37. http://dx.doi.org/10.1525/aa.2004.106.2.225.

Walsh, Andrew. 2005. "The Obvious Aspects of Ecological Underprivilege in Ankarana, Northern Madagascar." *American Anthropologist* 107 (4): 654–65. http://dx.doi.org/10.1525/aa.2005.107.4.654.

Walsh, Andrew. 2006. "'Nobody Has a Money Taboo': Situating Ethics in a Northern Malagasy Sapphire Mining Town." *Anthropology Today* 22 (4): 4–8. http://dx.doi.org/10.1111/j.1467-8322.2006.00447.x.

Walsh, Andrew. 2007. "Ethnographic Alchemy: Perspectives on Anthropological Work from Northern Madagascar." In *Anthropology Put to Work*, ed. Les Field and Richard G. Fox, 201–16. Oxford: Berg Publishers.

Walsh, Andrew. 2009. "The Grift: Getting Burned in the Northern Malagasy Sapphire Trade." In *Economics and Morality: Anthropological Approaches*, ed. Kate Brown and Lynne Milgram, 59–76. Lanham, MD: Altamira Press.

Walsh, Andrew. 2010. "The Commodification of Fetishes: Telling the Difference between Natural and Synthetic Sapphires." *American Ethnologist* 37 (1): 98–114. http://dx.doi.org/10.1111/j.1548-1425.2010.01244.x.

Walsh, Andrew. 2012. "After the Rush: Living with Uncertainty in a Malagasy Mining Town." *Africa* 82 (2): 235–51. http://dx.doi.org/10.1017/S0001972012000034.

West, Paige. 2006. *Conservation Is Our Government Now: The Politics of Ecology in Papua New Guinea*. Durham, NC: Duke University Press.

West, Paige. 2012. *From Modern Production to Imagined Primitive: The Social World of Coffee from Papua New Guinea*. Durham, NC: Duke University Press.

West, Paige, and James Carrier. 2004. "Ecotourism and Authenticity: Getting Away From It All?" *Current Anthropology* 45 (4): 483–98. http://dx.doi.org/10.1086/422082.

Wikipedia. N.d. "Madagascar." http://en.wikipedia.org/wiki/Madagascar.

Wildlife Conservation Society. N.d. "Madagascar: Island of Megadiversity." Wild Explorations. http://www.wildexplorations.com/home/18763581/madagascar-about.html.

Wilson, Jane M., Paul D. Stewart, and Simon V. Fowler. 1988. "Ankarana: A Rediscovered Nature Reserve in Northern Madagasar." *Oryx* 22 (3): 163–71. http://dx.doi.org/10.1017/S0030605300027794.

Wolf, Eric. 1982. *Europe and the People Without History*. Berkeley: University of California Press.

Wollenberg, Katharina C., Richard K.B. Jenkins, Roma Randrianavelona, Roseline Rampilamanana, Mahefa Ralisata, Andrianirina Ramanandraibe, Olga Ramilijaona Ravoahangimalala, and Miguel Vences. 2011. "On the Shoulders of Lemurs: Pinpointing the Ecotouristic Potential of Madagascar's Unique Herpetofauna." *Journal of Ecotourism* 10 (2): 101–17. http://dx.doi.org/10.1080/14724049.2010.511229.

Zola, Emile. 2008 [1885]. *Germinal*, trans. Peter Collier. Oxford: Oxford University Press.

Zrobowski, Megan. 2007. "Brands Rising." *Colored Stone* 21 (1): 22–25.

INDEX

Abdou, 32
affective value, 98–99
Ambondromifehy
  boom and immigration to, 14–19, 25
  daily life, 44–48
  description, xix–xx, 14–16
  ethos changes, 18
  exchanges in, 37–38
  foreigners and tourists in, xix–xx
  gifting, 38–39
  investment in, 29
  miners in, 28, 29–31
  sacred tree and places, 16–17
  sapphires in, xix–xx, xxii
  speculation about tourists, 66–67, 69
  trade organization, 33
  uncertainties, 104–105, 106
  women, 32–33
American Gem Trade Association (AGTA),
  79–80
ampanjaka, 4, 6, 7, 11
Ankarana. *See also* Antankarana
  anthropological research, xxix–xxx, 22
  benefits of ecotourism, 53–55
  description, 8–9
  foreigners' interest in, 1–2, 8–9
  French in, 8–9
  in global bazaar and economy, xxv–
    xxvi, 76–77, 103
  globalization, effect, 20–21
  guides' knowledge, 58–59
  house building, 29

immigration to, 13–14
maps of, 1–2
meaning to Antankarana, 2–12
as natural wonder, 8–13
opportunity in, 13–20
protection, 3, 7–8, 9–13
representation and online facts,
  xviii–xix
as sacred place, 3–7
Ankarana massif, description, xviii–xix
Ankarana National Park
  authenticity and, 96–97
  cultural differences in interpretation,
    68–69
  description and popularity, 49–50
  ecotourism, 49–50, 90–91
  expectations of ecotourists, 90–92
  for foreign visitors, xx, 70–71
  guides, 56–57, 58–59
  highway signs about, 70–71
  illegal activities, 63–64
  local visitors, 70–71
  mining, xxii, xxix–xxx, 14, 17–18, 19
  as natural wonder, 49
  protection, 9–12
  reasons to visit, 47–48, 69–70
  research projects, 50–51, 59–60
  roads, 56–57
  sapphires, xx, xxii, xxix–xxx, 19, 63–64
  speculation about tourists, 65–67, 69
  taboos, 11
  threats to, 9–10, 13

121

tourists numbers, 55–56
value, 9–12, 74–75, 86–87
visitors access, 52
Ankarana Special Reserve, 9, 52. *See also*
Ankarana National Park
Anne, 66, 94, 96
Antankarana. *See also* local people
affiliations, 3–4
benefits from conservation, 11–12
foreign travel, 70
as guides, 59
kingdom and rulers, 4, 6
meaning of Ankarana to, 2–12
research about, xix
in tourism, 11–12
anthropology
Ankarana and, xxix–xxx, 22
description, xxviii–xxix
globalization and, 21–22
in Madagascar, xxvii–xxviii
methods and practices, 110–112
prospective play, 110–111
speculations about, 108–109
use and value of, 107
Antsiranana, foreign buyers, 36–37
Attenborough, David, 87
authenticity, 95–97

Bandy, Joe, 54
Batchelor, Rev. R.T., 8, 9
bazaar economy, xxvi–xxvii. *See also*
global bazaar
Beesley, C.R., 83
Befourouack, Julien, 9, 10
Bera, 109, 111–112
biodiversity
description and value, 87–89
ecotourism for, xxiv
research projects, 50–51
sapphire extraction, xxx
threats to, 9–10, 13
tourist numbers, 55–56
blessings, 5–6, 17
buyers and sellers, interaction and
deception, 34–36, 40–41

Cardiff, Scott, 9, 10
Carrier, James, 90
cattle herding, 64

chameleons, 85–86
Clement, Mily, 10–11
coffee, 102–103
commodities
authenticity and, 95–97
conflicts of interest, 103–104
global trade, 23–24
natural wonders, 93–97
one-of-a-kind value, 95–96
value and, 102–103
confidence, in gifting and grifting, 39–40
conflicts of interest, 103–104
conservation
Ankarana, 3, 7–8, 9–13
Ankarana National Park, 9–12
benefits for local population, 11–13
ecotourism and, 51, 72
vs. ethos of growth, 13
illegal activities and, 64
support from rulers, 11, 51–52
consumption habits, 30–31
corundum, 78–79. *See also* sapphires and
sapphire trade
credit, deception through, 41–43
crocodiles, 10
cultural differences, 68–69
customs, in Antankarana kingdom, 5–6

Dadilahy, 1–2, 3–4
dare, 26–28
deception, 39–41
demantoid, 105
Duffy, Rosaleen, 89–90

earnings, from mining, 28–30
ecotourism. *See also* natural wonders;
tourists
Ankarana National Park as destination,
49–50, 90–91
authenticity and, 96–97
benefits from, xxvi, 53–55, 61, 71–72,
76–77, 86, 104
biodiversity and, xxiv
business of, xxii–xxiv
case studies, 53, 54
consequences, xxiii–xxiv
conservation and, 51, 72
development and promotion, xxiii–
xxiv, 51–53, 58, 75–76, 88–90

online, xv–xvi, xvii–xviii, xxvii
in sapphire trade, xxvi, 33–35, 37, 42–43,
46–47
through guide work, 60, 62, 65
value of, 42–43
international trade. *See* global economy
investment
for the future, 29, 31
in sapphires, 32

Jao, risks and dare, 25–29, 30, 31, 38–39
jewellery, 45–46, 47, 78, 80–81
Joan, 91–92

Keller, Eva, 5, 13
kingdom for Antankarana, 4–6
knowledge differentials, 33–34, 46–47. *See
also* information
Koko
gifting, 38–39
risks and dare, 25, 27, 29, 30, 31
Krüger, Oliver, 55

landscape, in Ankarana history, 4
language of tourists and foreigners, 58
Lindholm, Charles, 95, 96
local people
benefits from ecotourism and sapphire
trade, xxv–xxvi, 53–55, 61, 71–72,
76–77, 86, 104
vs. foreigners, 109
in global bazaar and trade, 23–24,
106–107
natural wonders and, 99
protection of Ankarana, 11–13
visit to Ankarana National Park, 70–71
luxuries, 46

MacCannell, Dean, 89
MacClancy, Jeremy, 110–111
Madagascar
history, xvi–xvii, 86–87
one-of-a-kind value, 87–90, 91
online facts, xv–xvi, xvii–xviii
political crises, 105–106
promotion of ecotourism and sapphire
trade, 75–76, 88–90
reciprocity custom, 38–39, 40, 42
research projects, 50–51

tourist numbers, 53
trade restrictions, 104–105
value of environment, 86–88
view of, xvii–xviii, 86–87
Madame Fernand, 41–43
Mahamasina
ecotourism, xxiii, 52–53, 54, 61
guides to Ankarana National Park,
56–57, 58–59
market uncertainties, 105–106
Malagasy people, xvii, 75
maps of Ankarana, 1–2
Marco Polo, 86–87
Maurer, David, 40
Mauss, Marcel, 38
media depiction of Madagascar, 87–88
Mineral Resources Governance Project
(MRGP), 75–76
mining and miners. *See also* sapphires
and sapphire trade
in Ankarana National Park, xxii, xxix–
xxx, 14, 17–18, 19
description, 25–26, 27, 81, 105
ecotourism and, 63–64
hot money, 28–30, 32
lifestyle of miners, 29–31
prospectors and immigration, 14
risking and daring, 25–28
work conditions, xxi
morengy, 28

National Environmental Action Plan
(NEAP), 10–11, 51, 52–53, 54, 75–76
natural resources, 75–76, 77
natural wonders. *See also* ecotourism;
sapphires and sapphire trade
Ankarana, 8–13
Ankarana National Park, 49
definition, 77, 93
effect on local people, 99
feelings about, 98–99
as market and commodity, xxvi–xxvii,
xxx, 93–97
one-of-a-kind value, 93–96, 97–98, 104
naturalness, 95–97
neoliberalism, 72
Nivo, 68, 69
Nosy Be, 57–58

INDEX

Omar, 37

one-of-a-kind value. *See also* value
    of commodities, 95–96
    concept, 77
    ecotourism, 77, 86, 91, 92–93
    Madagascar, 87–90, 91
    natural wonders, 93–96, 97–98, 104
    sapphires, 77, 83–84, 92–93

online information, xv–xvi, xvii–xviii,
    xxvii

opportunities, in Ankarana, 13–20

outsiders. *See* foreigners

paradox of plenty, 76

Pietz, William, 97

population growth, and conservation, 13

prospective play, 109–111

protection. *See* conservation

reciprocity, 38, 40, 42

reputability of miners, 30

Réserve Spéciale d'Ankarana, 9, 52. *See
    also* Ankarana National Park

resource curse, 76

risks, 25–31, 36, 61–62

roads to Ankarana National Park, 56–57

Robert, 57–66, 70, 75

Roby, 33, 35

"the rocks," description, xviii–xix

rulers
    French settlers and administrators, 9
    inviting foreigners to events, 7, 11
    in kingdom for Antankarana, 4, 6

ruses and ploys, 41–42

sacred tree and places in
    Ambondromifehy, 16–17

sacredness, of Ankarana, 3–7

sapphires and sapphire trade. *See also*
    mining and miners; natural wonders
    in Ambondromifehy, xix–xx, xxii
    authenticity, 95–96
    benefits from, xxv–xxvi, 76–77, 104
    buying and selling, 32–37
    corundum, 78–79
    descriptive terms for, 34
    earnings from, 28–30, 33–34
    ecotourism and, xx, xxv, xxx, 63–64, 73
    finishing into gemstones, 82–83

foreigners and, 23–24, 36–37, 43
gifting and grifting, 37–43
in global economy, xx–xxii, 23–24,
    76–77, 78, 80–81, 83–84
government development of, 75–76,
    88–90
immigration rush, 14–16
information about, xxvi, 33–35, 37,
    42–43, 46–47
investment in, 32
laboratory production, 79
natural *vs.* synthetic, 79–81, 83, 93–94
one-of-a-kind value, 83–84, 92–93
qualities and characteristics, 34–35,
    78–79, 83–84
risking and daring, 25–31
sieving and panning, 26
source, 80–82, 84
trade restrictions, 104–105
triage, 35
trunk shows, 80–81
uncertainties, 104–105, 106
use for, xix–xx, 36, 78–79, 93–94
value, xx, 84, 94, 104
women in, 32–33

sellers and buyers, interaction and
    deception, 34–36, 40–41

Sodikoff, Genese, 64

speculation
    tourists and ecotourism, 65–71
    use of sapphires, 45–48

Starbucks, 101

status, and dare, 28

surface-diffusion treatment, 82–83

taboos, 5–7, 11, 17–18

Thailand, 37, 42–43, 82

Thompson, Sharon Elaine, 83

tour operators, 54–55, 56–57, 61

tourism. *See* ecotourism

tourists. *See also* ecotourism
    authenticity and, 96–97
    behaviour, 57–58, 62–63, 66–68, 85–86,
        92
    numbers of, xxiii–xxiv, 55–56
    promotion of Madagascar, 88–89
    speculation about, 65–69
    value for, 86, 92